Thrasher's Fly Fishing Guide

An Essential Handbook for All Skill Levels

D1302187

Praise for *Thrasher's Fly Fishing Guide*

"No matter where you are in your evolution as a fly fisher, Susan's passion for her daily life as a teacher and guide gives a sense of your having been there with her, even as she leads you to ever-more-enjoyable stages of this lifetime sport."

—*Joan Wulff, founder, Wulff School of Fly Fishing*

"This fly fishing guide is a brilliant escape from the stuffy tutorials often found in the fishing world. Told through real-life stories, the author's passion and love of bringing new anglers into the fold is overshadowed only by her true dedication to the sport itself. This is a literary gem bound to become a pillar in today's fly fishing landscape."

—*Jen Ripple, editor,* Dun Magazine

"This book is enjoyable for the angler and adventurer alike. It is packed with information that is easy to learn and understand. Within the adventures, Susan conveys the camaraderie of fellow fisherman and the bond of women learning a male-dominated sport. She has the ability to make you feel that you were with her on the adventure. Her depth of knowledge and her concern for her fellow fishermen is evident in each story. This is a great book that you will likely read over and over."

—*Sheila Hassan, director, Wulff School of Fly Fishing*

"If fly fishing has had you curious but baffled, Susan's stories will unlock its mysteries. As an astute fly fishing guide, she shares her on-land and rowing-water tales that compel you to read and learn! From the cast to the fish, you'll want this book as a keeper!"

—*Lori-Ann Murphy, cofounder, Reel Women*

"Once one takes a fly rod into their hands and casts into the moving streams, and makes that cast that lifts and presents a beautiful fly into the open mouth of a fish—boom! You are hooked forever. And Susan is the one to teach you. Not only is she talented, smart, and beautiful—oh! and magical—she can teach us to fish. My sister, Becky, and I have seen her river, had a cup of tea with her, and viewed the vintage trailers she used for guests. Now my only job left is to fish with her."

—*Maurrie Sussman, founder and president, Sisters on the Fly*

Thrasher's Fly Fishing Guide

An Essential Handbook for All Skill Levels

S<small>USAN</small> T<small>HRASHER</small>

MENASHA RIDGE PRESS
www.menasharidge.com
Your Guide to the Outdoors Since 1982

Thrasher's Fly Fishing Guide: An Essential Handbook for All Skill Levels
Susan Thrasher
Copyright © 2020 by Susan Thrasher
All rights reserved
Published by Menasha Ridge Press
Distributed by Publishers Group West
Printed in the United States of America
First edition, second printing 2020

Project editor: Kate Johnson
Cover design: Scott McGrew
Text design: Annie Long
Interior photos: Susan Thrasher except where noted on page
Proofreader: Rebecca Henderson
Indexer: Rich Carlson
Front cover photo by Susan Thrasher
Back cover photo: © Rocksweeper/Shutterstock

FSC
MIX
Paper
FSC® C011935

Library of Congress Cataloging-in-Publication Data

Names: Thrasher, Susan, 1962– author.
Title: Thrasher's fly fishing guide : an essential handbook for all skill levels / Susan Thrasher.
Other titles: Fly fishing guide
Description: Birmingham, AL : Menasha Ridge Press, [2019] | Summary: "Fly fishing is a
    wonderful and thrilling way to catch fish—and it isn't as complicated as you might
    think. More and more people are casting fly rods and catching trout, bluegill, sailfish,
    and more. You can count yourself among them. It just takes the right equipment, a
    little bit of know-how, and some practice. If you've never tried because you heard it's
    'too hard,' then you are missing out! Ignore the doubters and the naysayers."
    —Provided by publisher.
Identifiers: LCCN 2019035886 (print) | LCCN 2019035887 (ebook) |
    ISBN 9781634042444 (pbk.) | ISBN 9781634042451 (ebook)
Subjects: LCSH: Fly fishing. | Fly fishing for women—United States.
Classification: LCC SH456 .T54 2019 (print) | LCC SH456 (ebook) |
    DDC 799.12/4082—dc23
LC record available at https://lccn.loc.gov/2019035886
LC ebook record available at https://lccn.loc.gov/2019035887

 MENASHA RIDGE PRESS
An imprint of AdventureKEEN
2204 First Ave. S, Ste. 102
Birmingham, Alabama 35233
800-443-7227; fax 205-326-1012

Visit menasharidge.com for a complete listing of our books and for ordering information. Contact us at our website, at facebook.com/menasharidge, or at twitter.com/menasharidge with questions or comments. To find out more about who we are and what we're doing, visit blog.menasharidge.com.

PERFECT

On a day like today
Everything else fades away
And the river washes me clean.
The sun on my skin
Warms my soul deep within
As I take in the beautiful scene.
When I'm almost enlightened,
The line comes tight and
A bright silver fish clears the water.
She darts and she dashes,
Dives, twists and splashes,
Then I reach with my net . . . and I've caught her!
On a day like today
Everything else fades away
As I put that fish back in the stream
With a whisper of thanks
To the fish and the banks
For helping me live the dream.

—Paul Grindlay

Table of Contents

OPPOSITE: THE AUTHOR WITH A RAINBOW TROUT CAUGHT USING THE EUROPEAN NYMPHING TECHNIQUE (SEE CHAPTER 32, PAGE 275) *Photographed by Leann Koleas*

Foreword

"The great charm of fly fishing is that we are always learn-
ing; no matter how long we have been at it, we are constantly
making some fresh discovery, picking up some new wrinkle."

—Theodore Gordon

IN HIS ESSAY "Starting Out," the celebrated author and fly fisher
Dana Storrs Lamb tells us that "whatever priceless item from the
beautiful bundle of a fishing trip especially delights one's heart, the
greatest of all is starting out, since therein is the entire treasure of
what may be to come." Beginnings, or "starting out," whether experienced by novice or veteran, are quite often among life's most exciting
moments, especially when one has a guide like Susan Thrasher leading
the way, which she does so well in this book.

We are fortunate Susan discovered her passion for fly fishing on
an outing with her father on Tennessee's South Holston River, where,
in her words, her casting that first day was "awful." But nothing could
deter her: smitten with the great joy she felt in fishing with the "long
rod" on that first outing, she readily became a convert.

For many years Susan braided her passion for a life on the water
with a successful career as an engineer while learning all she could
about the intricacies of fly fishing. Eventually, in the spirit of Izaak
Walton's *The Compleat Angler*, she saw a need to set "aside business" in
favor of her growing passion for going "a-fishing." Fortunately, her
plan included taking us along.

So, after hearing Susan deliver an extremely well-organized and
informative presentation on fly fishing at a meeting of the Northern Kentucky Fly Fishers (NKFF), I introduced myself and suggested

she consider writing a book. Luckily for all of us, she thought the idea intriguing. The next morning, over coffee and doughnuts, along with NKFF's Tim Guilfoile, we met with Richard Hunt, president of AdventureKEEN, and he readily agreed. And so, *Thrasher's Fly Fishing Guide* was officially hatched.

The information in this guide comes from Susan's years of teaching both new and seasoned anglers the art and techniques of fly fishing, primarily through her Nashville-based guide service, Southern Brookies, and as one of only seven instructors at the highly respected Wulff School of Fly Fishing, located on the legendary Beaverkill River in New York's Catskill Mountains, the birthplace of fly fishing in America.

Thrasher's Fly Fishing Guide is a singular treasure of a handbook: it offers the essential and sometimes overwhelming how-to details of fly fishing with the crystal clarity of a trout stream, infused with an abundance of knowledge acquired through years of guiding and teaching, both on and off the water. Susan's students—I count myself proudly among them—appreciate her kind heart, welcoming smile, and natural ability as a teacher.

Keep this handbook close, as you will come to rely on the wisdom it contains. And if you are lucky enough to spend time with Susan around the water, you will witness how those "awful" casts of yesteryear are a far toss from the lovely ones she unfurls today.

—*Ron Ellis*
Kentucky
October 2019

RON ELLIS IS the author of *Cogan's Woods* and *Brushes with Nature: The Art of Ron Van Gilder* and editor of *In That Sweet Country: Uncollected Writings of Harry Middleton* and *Of Woods & Waters: A Kentucky Outdoors Reader.* He is a contributor to the anthologies *Astream: American Writers on Fly Fishing, Afield: American Writers on Bird Dogs,* and *A Passion for Grouse: The Lore and Legend of America's Premier Game Bird.* His stories have appeared in *Sporting Classics, Kentucky Afield, Kentucky Monthly,* and *The Journal of Kentucky Studies,* among others. He is the recipient of the Kentucky Arts Council's Al Smith Individual Artist Fellowship and Professional Assistance Award. He lives in his native Kentucky.

THE MUSIC CITY FLY GIRLS IN ALBERTA, CANADA

Introduction

I HAVE SET MANY goals for myself, some of which I have been fortunate enough to achieve. Writing a book, however, was never, ever on the list. It's funny how small events can turn into big opportunities. Some people call it luck, some call it coincidence; I call it providence. Here is a prime example: I accepted an invitation to give a presentation to the Northern Kentucky Fly Fishers, a fly fishing club in Burlington, Kentucky, near Cincinnati. It was a great evening with a wonderful group of people, all sharing the passion of fly fishing. Following my talk, a very kind fellow named Ron Ellis, who has since become a dear friend, presented me with a surprising challenge. Ron stated frankly, "You should write a book." I let him know that I had written a few short articles here and there but never considered myself an author by any stretch of the imagination. He continued to persuade me, saying he had a close friend who was a publisher and, if I could stick around an extra day, he would like to set up a meeting at the publisher's bookstore, which also doubled as a bakery and coffee shop. Now, that got my attention! Coffee is one of my top three favorite things in life. I also love doughnuts, so I agreed to go.

Fast-forward, and here I am with something I had no idea could ever happen. There are thousands of very well-written books on fly fishing covering every aspect of the sport imaginable, so the task of finding my place among these great works was a daunting thought. I've always found myself captivated by people discussing topics they are truly passionate about. With this in mind, my approach to writing this book has been to let the words flow naturally, based on ideas and topics that inspire the greatest passion in me. I love teaching the art of fly fishing and especially enjoy seeing people progress along their journey as they become better anglers and more confident in their abilities. So, as I attempt to contribute to the fly fishing library, my goal is to share some of the "on the water" experiences of fly fishing that I have learned along the way. Between these covers, I've reflected on friendships, adventures, challenges, extreme happiness, sorrow, hope, and encouragement. The how-to guides and information are wrapped in treasured memories from my time as cofounder of the Music City Fly Girls; instructor at the Wulff School of Fly Fishing; and owner of my small business, Southern Brookies. My hope is threefold: A reader with no interest in fishing can enjoy the story thread weaving through the chapters, a beginning fly fisher will see the proverbial light bulb brighten, and the most advanced angler will find a few nuggets of information that haven't yet reached his or her sphere of learning.

One of my favorite things about fly fishing is the fact that there is always something new to learn. If I can teach you, the reader, a thing or two, sharing a little of my fly fishing passion and enticing you to get outdoors or, perhaps, placing a spiritual stone in your shoe, then I will have met the goal I set for myself.

CHAPTER 1

You Have to Start Somewhere

I HAVE LOVED THE outdoors all my life—camping, hiking, biking, fishing, I love it all. But some of my earliest childhood memories are from fishing with my dad. I can remember many summers spent visiting my grandparents in Mobile, Alabama. Daddy and I would slip off to Gulf Shores or to fish on the Fairhope Pier. We would make a stop by a little bait shack and pick up some fresh shrimp for the trip. I remember one time in particular when we were fishing in the surf on Dauphin Island. I kept running back up to the beach to get a new piece of shrimp when my bait would either come off or be nibbled up by a fish. Daddy told me to just stuff my pockets with shrimp to save me a trip back and forth, so that's exactly what I did. I recently reminded him of this, asking, "What were you thinking?" Yikes! Thinking of this now makes me realize we were sitting targets as shark bait.

Then there was the fishing trip that changed it all. A good family friend, Robert Shiver, invited us to join him for some fly fishing on the South Holston River in Bristol, Tennessee. I borrowed some oversize waders from a coworker and met up with Robert for a quick casting lesson before heading out to the water. My dad continues to remind me that my casting that first day was awful. I kept slapping the water behind me and overpowering the cast, but somehow I managed to catch my first trout. It was amazing. I still remember standing under the bridge, where the current was rushing around the bridge pier. I let the fly swing into the current and suddenly felt the tug of a trout taking the fly. It was so exciting. With the lightweight rod, I could feel every wiggle of the fish as I quickly stripped in the line to take a look at my first-ever catch on a fly rod. I only caught one that day, but that's all it took. That evening, my mom asked if we enjoyed our day fishing, and I told her that I was pretty certain the day had changed my life. I wanted to learn everything I possibly could about this thing called fly fishing. That was the beginning of a passion that has continued to grow in intensity over the past 20 years.

Since then, I've had the opportunity to share my fly fishing passion with hundreds of folks. One of the things I hear so often is, "It looks so complex. I don't have any idea where to even start." It certainly can be overwhelming and intimidating, but the secret is to take it one step at a time.

Let's take a look at the basics of fly fishing and how conventional fishing differs in many ways. We will unpack these items in greater detail in subsequent chapters.

● **FLIES** One of the greatest things about fly fishing is the fact that you don't use any live or stinky bait. The term *bait* isn't used in fly fishing. The bait is referred to as a fly, and it's made from natural and synthetic materials. Flies are organized in categories such as nymphs, larvae, pupae, emergers, dry flies, and streamers. These terms reference the life-cycle stages of the insects or other food sources, such as small bait fish or crustaceans, that the flies are imitating.

ARTIFICIAL FLIES AVOID THE MESS OF TRADITIONAL BAIT.

A NATURAL CADDIS LARVA AND ITS IMITATION

A NATURAL STONE FLY AND ITS IMITATION

A NATURAL MAYFLY NYMPH AND ITS IMITATION

● **FLY ROD** First off, it's called a fly rod, not a pole. Fly fishers can get a little snobby about some things, and this is one of them. Rods come in a range of lengths, sizes, flexes, materials, and prices. These days it's hard to find a bad fly rod. The cost difference will primarily be based on the materials used.

FLY RODS COME IN A VARIETY OF LENGTHS AND WEIGHTS FOR DIFFERENT FISHING SITUATIONS.

● **REEL** The reel isn't permanently fixed to the rod. It is screwed on and off with each use and sits just below the rod grip. The reel handle will typically be placed on the opposite side of the dominant hand. For example, if you are right-handed, the reel handle will be on the left side. This is referred to as left-hand retrieve. So, when you hook a fish, you don't have to change hands to reel it in. This isn't a hard-and-fast rule, but it's typical for most anglers.

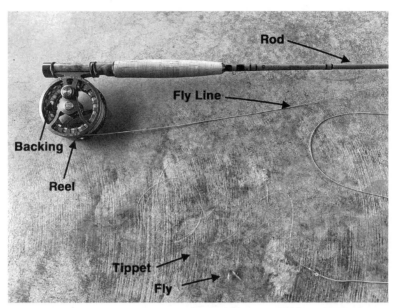

A FLY ROD, LINED AND READY TO FISH

• **BACKING** Before you attach the fly line to the reel, a length of backing will need to be spooled onto it. Backing is a strong, yet thin, material made out of Dacron or polyester, which looks a lot like kite string. The backing serves two purposes: It bulks up the spool diameter so the line isn't wound too tightly around the spool reel itself, which would result in tight coils. It also serves as insurance. A typical fly line is 90 feet long. If you hook into a large fish that takes off running on you and takes out all 90 feet of line, then you may be out of luck without the extra length of attached backing to continue fighting the fish.

• **FLY LINE** In very simplistic terms, fly line is tightly braided fishing line covered with a plastic coating. There are various profiles, colors, and weights. Some fly lines float, some sink like a rock, and some sink just a little. The line you select will depend on your fishing conditions, the type of water you are fishing, and the type of fish you will be hunting.

- **LEADER** The leader is attached to the end of the fly line. It is typically clear and made of nylon or fluorocarbon. You can use manufactured tapered leaders known as knotless leaders or construct your own, tying together various lengths and diameters of material, from a thick diameter (where it attaches to the fly line) down to a thin diameter (where the fly attaches).

- **TIPPET** The tippet is the section of nylon or fluorocarbon material where the fly is attached. It can be the very end of a manufactured tapered leader or the final section of a knotted leader.

- **CASTING** Casting a fly rod is completely different from casting a conventional fishing rod. With conventional tackle, you are casting the weight of the sinker, lure, or bait. The weight is propelled forward, and the fishing line is pulled out from the reel. With fly fishing, you are casting the weight of the fly line itself. The leader, tippet, and fly travel along as a passenger. I used to think if I tied on a heavily weighted fly that I could really get it out there. Not so. The heavier fly is actually harder to cast since it has wind resistance. Just remember, heavier passenger, harder to cast. The trick is letting your rod do all the work. I find that women oftentimes pick up the art of fly fishing a little faster than men. This is because men tend to use more muscle and overpower the cast, where women seem to understand the importance of adding softness or finesse to the casting stroke. Once you understand that it's more about a smooth stroke than about muscle, you are halfway there. For more on Casting, see page 281.

- **CATCHING** Most people who are new to fly fishing have the idea that fly fishing is only for trout. Thankfully, this isn't the case. Any fish you can catch with the conventional rod can also be caught with a fly rod. From bluegill to sailfish, I personally believe it's much more fun with a fly rod.

Where Should I Begin?

YOU CAN DO a lot of reading about casting a rod or tying a knot, but I have found the best way to learn is by taking a lesson or going through a beginning fly fishing school. There's no substitute for hands-on instruction. Sure, it's an investment, but trust me, I tried teaching myself and know firsthand the frustration I could have avoided by getting a good foundation from an instructor. You want to learn the right way from the beginning. Otherwise, as with casting, you may practice incorrect methods and develop muscle memory that will be difficult, although not impossible, to undo.

There are a number of learning options available to get started. Most instructors and guides have their own equipment, so all you will need to do is show up. You can take a short lesson or a day- or week-end-long instructional course, or you can dive in headfirst and go on a fly fishing trip with a guide and simply learn as you go. This latter option is the hard way. I personally believe taking a casting lesson beforehand will make the trip much more enjoyable and less frustrating. If you live in an area with an Orvis store, give them a call. Most offer a free introductory class. It's very basic, but it's a great way to get your feet wet. There are even a number of community colleges or recreation centers that offer inexpensive classes as well. From there, you can move on to a more focused and intense class.

As an example, I offer a beginning class at my fly fishing school, Southern Brookies. It's a full day of total immersion into fly fishing. We cover a lot of material over a 6-hour period, so a student may not catch it all the first time. But having an initial exposure to the material is important. These are small classes with a maximum size of six students, which gives plenty of one-on-one time. It also gives enough time for students to try out casts on their own without an instructor constantly hovering over them. In addition to the casting instruction, we also cover equipment and setup; the necessary gear, such as vests, packs, waders, and boots; and a simplistic overview of entomology and the flies. One of the best sessions of the day is trying out different rods around the casting pond. Having an understanding of the various rod flexes, weights, and lengths is an important part of the fly fishing education. We end the day by learning the knots you will need for tying the leader to the fly line and the tippet to the leader, and also how to tie on the fly. The goal of the class is to give students enough information that they can knowledgeably begin to select their own equipment and then venture out on their own and fish independently.

If you aren't into group learning, then you may be better off scheduling a private session. A private lesson with a qualified instructor can be customized to fit your individual needs. If you are looking for an instructor in your area, check out Fly Fishers International (FFI). The organization focuses on conservation and education. FFI's instructor program started in 1992 to help casting instructors with their teaching ability and overall knowledge of fly fishing. If you hire a certified instructor, you can be assured they have gone through rigorous training and testing to ensure they are ready to teach others. I personally have gone through the Casting Instructor Certification Program (CICP) and can vouch for the rigor!

Many of the students I have taught have been intimidated to begin fly fishing. Just remember, we all started out as beginners. Everyone starts out with limited knowledge and throwing a tangle or two. The important part is to start out with a desire to learn. One of the best parts of fly fishing is the lifelong learning the sport offers. There is always some new aspect to learn. You just have to take a step forward and begin.

CHAPTER 2

Gear to Get You Started

WILL ADMIT TO being a gear nut. I've always been that way. My mom and sister can tell you that I am able to sniff out an outdoors shop no matter where we are in the world. They have watched it happen many times. So, after that initial South Holston fly fishing trip with my dad, I knew that I had to get some gear of my own. I couldn't wait until my first visit to a fly shop. I was living in Virginia Beach at the time, so I took a short weekend trip to the town of Lexington, Virginia, and stumbled upon a little fly shop called Reel Time Outfitter. The owner of the shop helped me select a 5-weight St. Croix rod, a reel, and a few other items. I hired him as a guide for the rest of the afternoon, fishing for smallmouth on a nearby river. I was so proud of that rod, and I still have it. That was the start of many, many more fly-shop visits and gear purchases.

As with any other sport, you can spend a boatload of money on gear, but it's certainly not required to have a great day of fly fishing. One question I am asked often by students who are just getting into fly fishing is about the gear and what essential items they need to get started. There are some high-quality, reasonably priced products out there these days, so it's hard to go wrong. What I'm including in this chapter are the items I've personally

WEIGHT-FORWARD
FLOATING FLY LINE

used and had success with. Let's take a look at the critical items that you will need.

● **FLY LINE** This is the heart and soul of your gear, so spend a little extra for a good line. If you take care of it, it will last for many seasons. An all-around fly line for trout or small, warm-water fish will be a 5- or 6-weight line with a weight-forward design. My personal favorite is the Wulff Triangle Taper. If you get the Signature Series, the line will be two-toned, so you will always know where the head tapers to the running line. You will learn more about taper designs and weights in Chapter 8 (page 75). Bottom line though, you must have a fly line to get started.

RECOMMENDATIONS:

- Orvis Hydros Trout (orvis.com)
- Wulff Triangle Taper Signature Series (royalwulff.com)

● **ROD** You need a rod that will balance the fly line. So, if you purchase a 5-weight line, then you will need a 5-weight rod. I strongly recommend casting the rod before buying it. Rods vary in weight,

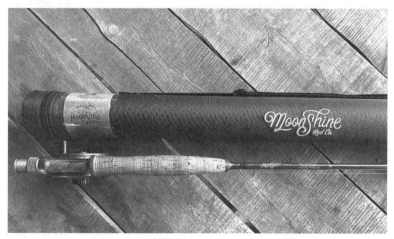

MOONSHINE 6-WEIGHT DRIFTER FLY ROD

length, flex, and grip size. You need a grip that fits your hand. If you get something too small or large, your hand could begin to cramp after a long day of casting. Most fly shops will let you step outside to cast a rod before it's purchased, so don't hesitate to ask. An all-around beginning fly rod is a 9-foot, 5- or 6-weight rod. You will learn more details about the various grip options and selecting a rod to fit your fishing conditions and casting style in Chapters 9 and 10 (pages 89 and 99, respectively).

RECOMMENDATIONS:

- Moonshine Drifter Series (moonshinerods.com)
- Orvis Clearwater Series (orvis.com)
- Temple Fork Outfitters Professional Series (tforods.com)

• **REEL** Unless you are going after some monster fish, the reel is basically a place to hold the fly line. You don't need to break the bank on a reel with your first purchase. Reels come in different sizes based on the size of the fly line you are using. As the weight of the fly line increases, the diameter increases, so the reel needs to match the line size. Most reels are sized to fit two or three sizes of line. For example, one reel could accommodate line sizes 1-, 2-, 3-, or 4-weight, or a reel could fit a 5- or 6-weight line, and so on. The line size that the reel will accommodate is typically shown on the box. Be

ORVIS BATTENKILL REEL

sure to wind on some backing before attaching the fly line. You can find a recommendation on the amount of backing to include from the reel manufacturer's website or ask the fly shop to do it for you. They have the equipment on hand to wind it quickly and efficiently.

RECOMMENDATIONS:

- Echo Base or Ion (echoflyfishing.com)
- Orvis Clearwater or Battenkill (orvis.com)
- Waterworks-Lamson Liquid (waterworks-lamson.com)

● **COMBO PACKAGE** There are a number of high-quality packages out there that include a rod, a reel, a fly line, a leader, and sometimes even a rod case, all for one price. This can be a great approach when you are on a budget and need a low-cost, high-quality package to get you started.

RECOMMENDATIONS:

- Echo Base Kit (echoflyfishing.com)
- Orvis Encounter Combo (orvis.com)
- Redington Path Combo (redington.com)

● **LEADER** You will need a package of knotless leaders. They come one or two to a package and typically come with a loop so you can easily attach it to the fly line with a loop-to-loop connection. If the loop isn't there, you will need to tie your own perfection loop or attach the leader to the fly line with a nail knot. These knots will be covered in Chapter 12 (page 113). Monofilament leaders will typically work; however, if the water is very clear and the trout are picky, you may need to invest in fluorocarbon leaders. They cost more, but the clarity does the trick when the fish are being finicky.

RECOMMENDATIONS:

- Cortland Nylon Tapered Leader (cortlandline.com)
- Orvis SuperStrong and Mirage Fluorocarbon (orvis.com)

KNOTLESS LEADERS ARE MANUFACTURED
TO TAPER DOWN SMOOTHLY, WHEREAS
KNOTTED LEADERS ARE TAPERED
MANUALLY USING TIPPET MATERIAL.

• **TIPPET** A spool or two of tippet will be necessary to ensure the tippet is the proper size for the fly you are using. You could get away with just having a leader, but eventually after tying on a number of flies and nipping off pieces of the leader, it will become too thick to thread through the eye of the hook. You will learn all about tippet sizes in Chapter 11 (page 107).

RECOMMENDATIONS:

  • Cortland Nylon (cortlandline.com)

  • Orvis SuperStrong and Mirage Fluorocarbon (orvis.com)

• **STRIKE INDICATORS** There are a number of options to choose from when it comes to strike indicators. They come in all shapes and sizes, from plastic stick-ons to yarn. However, I have found Air-Lock indicators to be the easiest to use and to see. The small screw top makes it easy to slide up and down the leader when changing depths. They come in a number of sizes, but I have found the 0.5-inch size works perfectly for most of the flies I use. You will learn more about the use of indicators in Chapter 3 (page 25). Be sure to add them to your shopping list.

RECOMMENDATIONS:

- Airflo Air-Lock Strike Indicator (0.5") (airflousa.com)
- New Zealand Wool Strike Indicator (strikeindicator.com)

● **FLIES** You will need a few flies before heading out to fish. Be sure to have at least two of each fly in your selection. There's nothing worse than finding a fly that works and then losing the fly in a tree on your backcast. I know this from my own unfortunate experience. See Chapter 23 (page 205) for some ideas and recommendations on flies.

● **FLY HOLDER** To keep your flies protected, you will need a container. You can use an old Altoids tin, a wine cork, or an actual fly box.

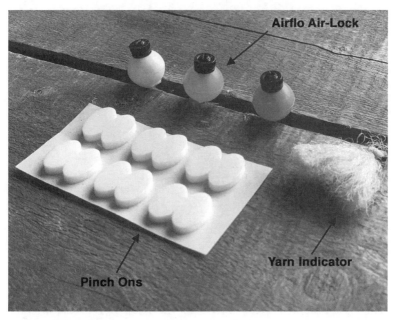

POPULAR STRIKE INDICATORS

There are many shapes and sizes to choose from, so, if you are like me, you will end up with a few before it's all over.

RECOMMENDATIONS:

- Montana Fly Company Poly Fly Box (montanafly.com)
- Fishpond Tacky Fly Box (fishpondusa.com)

FLY BOX AND LANYARD WITH NIPPERS, TIPPET SPOOLS, AND HEMOSTATS

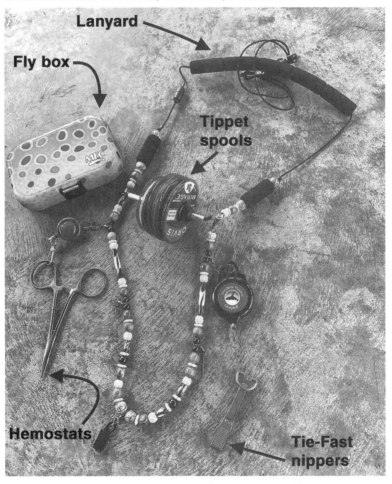

- **NIPPERS** It's tempting to use your teeth to bite off a piece of tippet, but it's not wise. While fingernail clippers can get you by for a while, they will eventually rust. Nippers aren't that expensive and are much cheaper than a dental visit to repair a chipped tooth.

RECOMMENDATIONS:

- Orvis Comfy Grip (orvis.com)
- Sierra Stream & Mountain Tie-Fast (scientificanglers.com)
- Umpqua River Grip (umpqua.com)

- **HEMOSTATS** Sometimes it's hard to get the fly out of the mouth of the fish. Since you want to do everything possible to release it safely and quickly, a pair of hemostats, or forceps, is essential. Some even have scissor blades built in for snipping off fly line or leader.

RECOMMENDATIONS:

- Montana Fly Company Hemostats (montanafly.com)
- Orvis Plier/Scissor Forceps (orvis.com)

Keeping It All Together

THERE ARE MANY ways to carry your gear, and you may end up using more than one type as you progress. Here are a few options:

- **LANYARD** If you want to take a minimalist approach, simply use a lanyard. A lanyard is basically a necklace with attachments for carrying your tippet and nippers, along with a few flies.

RECOMMENDATIONS:

- Dr. Slick Neck Lanyard (drslick.com)
- Loon Outdoors (loonoutdoors.com)
- Morning Star Lanyards (mslanyards.com)
- Nice Pack Co. (nicepack.storeenvy.com)

• **PACK** Packs come in all shapes and sizes. Waist, sling, chest, and combo packs are available in a variety of colors and designs. Some are waterproof, and some have a built-in fly box.

RECOMMENDATIONS:

- Orvis Safe Passage Sling Pack (orvis.com)
- Patagonia Stormfront Hip Pack (patagonia.com)

A NICE PACK CO. LANYARD FULLY LOADED

• **VEST** This is the classic approach to carrying your gear. There's plenty of room for your stuff, including a rain jacket and a bottle of water.

RECOMMENDATIONS:

- Filson Foul Weather Strap Vest (filson.com)
- Fishpond Mesh Vest (fishpondusa.com)
- Simms Freestone Fishing Hip Pack (simmsfishing.com)

• **WADING APPAREL** If you are fishing in the summer, you can get away with wearing shorts or quick-dry pants and some water shoes. However, if you plan to fish year-round, you will want to invest in some waders and boots. This is a must-have for chilly or rainy days. See Chapter 7 (page 65) for wader options and recommendations.

• **WADING BELT** When you purchase waders, they will come with a wading belt. However, you may want to look into Fishpond's

Westbank Wading Belt (fishpondusa.com). It has a holster to hold your net and webbing for other attachments.

• **SUNGLASSES** Polarized sunglasses are an essential piece of gear for two reasons. First of all, with a fly hovering overhead during each cast, you need to protect your eyes. Second, they reduce the reflected glare from the water, allowing you to see below the surface. This will enable you to see not only fish but also any obstacle that may be in your way as you are fishing.

RECOMMENDATIONS:
- Costa Del Mar (costadelmar.com)
- Maui Jim (mauijim.com)

These are the essential items you will need to get started. Obviously, as with any hobby, you will find additional equipment that will be useful on the water as you progress. But for now, keeping it simple will add to the pure enjoyment of those first trips to the water.

THE FISHPOND WESTBANK WADER BELT CAN BE USED WHEN WET WADING OR WITH YOUR WADERS. IT'S GREAT FOR HOLDING YOUR NET AND OTHER ATTACHMENTS.

CHAPTER 3

Fly Fishing Techniques

After that first day of fly fishing the South Holston and with the purchase of my new gear, I became completely hooked and wanted to spend all my time on the water. I'd only had success with a woolly bugger, so that's what I was fishing most of the time. I didn't know about the different techniques based on feeding patterns or hatches, so some days I came home skunked and a little frustrated. Little did I know that my fly fishing knowledge was about to expand rapidly.

I was working as a civil engineer with Parsons Brinckerhoff, and we had just landed a big roadway project in Salt Lake City, Utah. I was the lead traffic engineer, and this required me to be on site for a good bit of time during the project. As good fortune would have it, the area had some beautiful trout streams and a fly shop within a mile of the project office. I stopped in for a visit and found out about the Middle Provo River, about an hour from where I was staying.

After work, I made my way to the river, put on my waders, and ventured into the water. I had only been fishing for a few minutes when I heard a voice say, "Hello, do you fish this river often?" I turned around to see a fly fisherman standing on the bank with a large black Newfoundland dog anchored at his side.

"No," I said. "This is my first time to fish here."

"Well," he said, "you won't find any fish there. They don't have any structure for protection. I've never seen a single fish where you are. If you want, you can follow me, and I'll show you a few spots."

I hopped right out and followed him like the Pied Piper the rest of the afternoon. Not only did he show me a few good fishing holes, but he also introduced me to several fishing techniques. This opened up a whole new fishing world for me. From that moment, I became obsessed with being on the water. I couldn't wait to finish work and make the drive through the canyon to get back to the river.

My newfound friend was Jim Smith. He was a local surveyor working in the area. He had a big white truck with a camper mounted

PRACTICING NEW TECHNIQUES ON UTAH'S MIDDLE PROVO RIVER *Photographed by Kim Council*

in the truck bed. After work, most days and on weekends, he would pull into the river-access point and set up camp. He was the quintessential trout bum, and I thought he hung the moon. He was a big man wearing a cowboy hat, with a long white beard and thick mustache stained a little brown above his lip from the Camel cigarettes he smoked. Picture Grizzly Adams, and you've got it. For some reason, he took me under his wing and began to teach me the art of fly fishing.

Fortunately, the roadway project kept me working in Salt Lake for over a year. I traveled back and forth from Nashville. Quite often, I would forgo the return weekend trip back to Nashville and either stay with my good friends Tim and Mari Dougherty or get a hotel room in Heber City so I could spend the time fishing with Jim. My fly fishing skills improved tremendously. Like a bunch of arrows in a quiver, his tutelage had armed me for any fishing situation.

Types of Flies

Having a knowledge of the various techniques to use and when to apply them can easily make or break the success of your day.

But before diving into the techniques, defining the various stages of the insects and the imitating fly will prove useful. The four main flies on the trout's diet are the mayfly, stone fly, caddis fly, and midge. The mayfly and stone fly undergo an incomplete metamorphosis. The stages are egg, nymph, and adult. Basically, the insect looks the same in its immature form as it does in the adult form, with one exception: the adult has wings. As the insect hatches or begins to shed its outer skeleton and the new winged adult begins to escape, it's known as an emerger. The caddis and midge are a bit different. They undergo a complete metamorphosis, where the adult takes on a completely different form than the immature insect. They go through a four-stage process: egg, larva, pupa, and adult. Remember the evolution from a caterpillar to a butterfly.

If you research the various flies that imitate these life stages, you may find varying definitions, and it can be confusing. However, to keep it simple, this is the way I have kept it straight in my mind: dry flies float on the surface of the water, wet flies imitate the state of emergence in the surface film, and nymphs and larvae are fished subsurface, typically deeper in the water column.

The various fishing techniques can be divided into two basic categories: top water and subsurface. The categories are broken down a bit further by varying where you fish within the water column and the action placed on the fly. These are the fishing techniques that I have used over the past 20 years, and they haven't let me down.

Dry Fly Technique

DRY FLY FISHING is, by far, the most visually exciting fly fishing technique of all. There's nothing like delicately landing the fly on the surface of the water and then watching as a fish comes to the surface and takes your offering. Whether it's a slow sip or a devouring,

ADAMS DRY FLY

splashy take, dry fly fishing is hard to beat. The flies used are made of buoyant materials, which helps to keep the fly floating on the surface. They can also be dressed with a waterproof coating or powder to help keep the fly floating cast after cast. For many fly fishers, this is fly fishing in its purest form. The dry fly imitates the adult caddis fly, stone fly, midge, or mayfly when fishing traditional patterns. Terrestrials such as ants, beetles, and grasshoppers are also very productive dry fly options.

Swinging Wet Flies

FISHING AN EMERGING nymph or pupa in the surface film is typically referred to as swinging wet flies. Some of the fly imitations are referred to as soft hackles (such as the Eat at Chuck's fly; see photo, page 212). They are made with a wing that is similar to the adult but not as buoyant, so they will not float on the surface. The surface-film area is 6 inches or so below the surface. As insects emerge from their subsurface habitat and morph into adults, they struggle to break through the surface of the water. Sometimes this requires a number of tries. This time of struggle is when the insects are most vulnerable, and the trout take full advantage of the easy meal. The secret to swinging wet flies is keeping a tight line as the fly moves through the current. This keeps you connected to the fly, and you don't lose the tactile feel of the take. When a fish takes the fly, there will be no mistaking the tug. It's an adrenaline rush for sure, and one of the most exciting ways to fish. It's a very simple technique to master, basically casting across the stream and allowing the fly to flow downstream. If you simply allow the current to take the fly, it's referred to as a dead drift. However, you can apply a slow twitch or retrieve to give it a little action. Quite often, the take occurs at the end of the swing as the fly is rising to the surface, and then *wham*—just like that, fish on!

Nymph Fishing

STUDIES SHOW THAT fish feed beneath the surface of the water 90% of the time, so including this technique will certainly increase your fishing success. This technique is referred to as nymphing. This is really a catchall term. You may use the nymphal form of aquatic insects such as mayflies or stone flies (see page 6 for photos), but you can also use the flies that imitate the larva of caddis flies and midges. With this technique, you normally will not be fishing by feel, nor will you see the fish take the actual fly since it will be deep in the water column. So, you need to be keenly aware of what is going on with your fly and leader beneath the surface. If you see any hesitation in the fly line or leader, or any unusual movement, you will need to immediately set the hook. It doesn't take but a split second for the fish to spit out the fly, so quick reflexes are key to this technique. The fish will typically be hanging near the bottom, so getting the fly down deep in the water column is important. This can be accomplished by incorporating lead or a weighted bead into the design of the fly, or by adding split shot or twist lead (see Glossary) to the leader. If you have trouble detecting when a fish takes the fly by watching the line and leader, a strike indicator can be used. I have joked with my students that an indicator could be considered a bobber, but fly fishers are much too sophisticated to call it by that name, so it is termed a strike indicator. But seriously, it really is more than just a bobber. The indicator is placed on the leader and is used to set the depth of your fly, to check the speed of the current to maintain the proper drift, and to detect the strike. The location of the indicator on the leader depends on the water depth you will be fishing. A good rule of thumb is to place the indicator up from the fly, a distance equal to 1.5 times the depth of the water. If the fly begins to drag the bottom, you can reposition the indicator to make it more shallow.

Tandem Rigs

A s THE NAME suggests, this involves fishing with more than one fly. Fishing a tandem rig is also commonly referred to as "fishing a dropper." There are a number of configurations and knots that can be used in creating the rig. However, the simple method I use involves these basic steps:

1. **Tie on your first fly** (known as the point fly) as you normally would when fishing a single fly.

2. **Take a separate piece of tippet** (12 inches to start), and tie a clinch knot in one end, forming an open loop. Before cinching it down, attach the open loop to the hook bend of the fly you just tied on, and then pull to tighten the knot.

3. **Tie on a second fly,** or the dropper, to the end of this extra length of tippet. It's as simple as that. You now have a tandem rig.

The combinations you can use with a tandem rig are endless. Choosing which combination to use depends on what you are trying to discover or imitate. For example, there are times when two nymphs can be used to test which color, size, or pattern the feeding trout prefer. Also, there are times a combination would be used to identify at what depth the fish are feeding within the water column. Sometimes the combination is based on the life-cycle stage of the fly. For example, you could use a dry fly as the point fly and an emerger as the dropper. In this case, the dry fly would float high on top of the water, while the dropper would be resting in the surface film. Often, it may appear that trout are sipping flies off the surface, when in fact the majority of fish are feeding on the emergers moving up through the water column. Using this setup covers both circumstances. When fishing a dry fly and a dropper, you can think of the dry fly as being an indicator. If the dry fly disappears, you know the trout has your subsurface fly. If the trout takes the strike indicator (dry fly), your chances of landing the fish have increased dramatically, as the indicator now has a hook! The key to using a dry fly as the indicator is to use a fly that is buoyant enough to stay afloat and not sink under the weight of the dropper.

One of my best memories of fishing this technique was on the Middle Provo with Jim. The Middle Provo is full of medium-size rocks that stick up above the surface of the river. As the water flows around the rock, it forms an eddy, or soft pocket of slow-moving water, that is a perfect place for a lazy fish to hang out while waiting on a morsel of food. I was set up with two flies: a grasshopper imitation, which is a very buoyant dry fly, and a Copper John, which is a weighted nymph fished below the surface. This setup is also known as a hopper dropper. The length of tippet between the hopper and the nymph was only 6 inches. I walked upstream for about a mile, casting just above each rock and allowing the current to

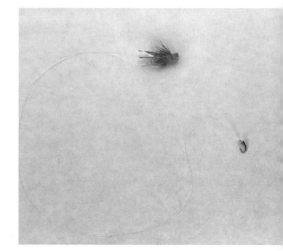

HOPPER DROPPER SETUP

move the hopper around the rock and drift into the pocket. With almost every cast, a trout would slam the hopper, or the hopper would quickly disappear, with the fish taking the Copper John. It was a very memorable day.

There are really no limits to your fly selection when fishing in tandem. You can try fishing two wet flies and swinging them through the current, or two weighted nymphs at varying distances apart. It's interesting to study the water and the feeding patterns and test different combinations until you discover a setup that works with the situation.

I suggest starting with 6–12 inches of tippet to the dropper until you get the feel for using the two-fly system. This is simply a starting point. As you progress, you will begin to recognize that the length of tippet between the two flies depends on two factors: the depth of water where you are fishing and where in the water column you want to position your fly. If you are fishing a deep, slow-moving pool, then the length of tippet between the two flies could be a few feet. If you are fishing a dry fly and a dropper through a riffle or shallow pocket of water, then a much shorter section is desirable. The length will vary based on the situation and what you are trying to accomplish.

When you first start fishing with more than one fly, be prepared for a few tangles. I can remember when I first started fly fishing and added on the dropper, I spent quite a bit of time picking out the rat's nest. You will need to be diligent about your good casting techniques. To avoid tangles, don't get lazy or sloppy. It's best to avoid tight loops when fishing more than one fly. Your loops will need to be slightly wider to avoid tangles.

Streamer Fishing

ANOTHER TECHNIQUE IN your arsenal should be fishing with streamers. Streamers are tied to resemble baitfish; leeches;

minnows; crayfish; and other long, slender food sources. They can be fished in a variety of ways: swinging through the current with no motion (dead drift) or short quick strips to look like darting, swimming, or escaping aquatic prey. It's best to try different retrieval speeds until you find what most entices the fish you are after. You will need to keep a tight connection with the fly so you can easily impart motion to it and so you can feel the strike. Keep in mind, the temperature may dictate the retrieval speed. In warm water, faster retrieves may be best, while cold weather requires a slower retrieve. Fish are more lethargic in cold temperatures and typically won't aggressively chase the fly.

Streamer fishing allows you to cover large areas of water quickly. You will often hear fly fishermen say things like "pounding the banks with streamers," "stripping streamers," or "slinging meat." This means they cast the fly close to shore, then retrieve and repeat.

The hook set is a little different than other techniques. Unlike dry fly or nymph fishing where you raise the rod tip to set the hook, with streamer fishing you apply a strip set. As you are stripping in the fly and feel the fish bump the fly, continue the strip to set the hook. Then you can lift the rod to finish the fight and land the fish.

You don't need as much stealth when fishing streamers as you do when using dry flies and nymphs because the fish are busy chasing down the flies and not paying as much attention to the leader. Use a short, stout leader, which will make it much easier to cast the

WOOLLY BUGGER

chunky, wind-resistant fly. So, leave the long, fine dry fly leader in your vest or pack. Read more about leaders in Chapter 11 (page 107).

As you can see, with all these techniques, it's hard to get bored during a day on the water fly fishing. You are constantly moving; changing techniques; and closely watching your line, leader, and fly. Finding a fly fishing mentor to help with some of these techniques can help your skills grow by leaps and bounds. I was so fortunate to meet my friend Jim on the river, as he turned out to be an amazing on-stream mentor. Most fly fishermen can't wait to share their fishing knowledge with newbies, so be on the lookout for that person who seems to be oozing with knowledge, and saddle up next to them. You won't be sorry.

CHAPTER 4

Getting the Most from Your Guided Trip

SPENDING THE DAY WITH LORI-ANN MURPHY (RIGHT) *Photographed by Carol Topping*

AFTER SPENDING MANY, many days throughout the year with Jim on the Middle Provo, I felt my skills were beginning to improve. I found myself reading about fly fishing techniques, beginning to tie flies, and getting the wild thought in my head of becoming an instructor and guide. I was a long way from having the skills to do it, but the desire and dream were there. Jim told me about two women I needed to contact about enrolling in their schools or classes. One was Lori-Ann Murphy, and the other, Joan Wulff. Since I was new to fly fishing, I wasn't familiar with them. I didn't realize the significance they held in the fly fishing world and would ultimately have on my fly fishing career and life overall.

That next summer, I was fortunate enough to be in Jackson Hole, Wyoming, so I decided to book a guide trip with Lori-Ann. Lori-Ann started Reel Women, and they were located just a short drive away in Victor, Idaho. I had a great day of fishing with Lori-Ann and told her about my dream to begin teaching and guiding. She suggested that I sign up for the Reel Women Guide School the next spring. This was a weeklong course covering the basics of guiding, including learning to row a drift boat, casting instruction, water safety, entomology, and other key topics. I felt it was the next obvious step in my journey, so I signed up for the May class. At the same time, I looked up Joan Wulff and found out about the Wulff School of Fly Fishing in the Catskills of New York. There were a number of schools to choose from, and I opted for a weekend-long casting school to improve my casting skills.

Both experiences far surpassed anything I was expecting. I came away with several important pieces of information. First, I suddenly realized I had only been exposed to the tip of the iceberg in learning about fly fishing. It was made obvious to me that fly fishing would be a lifelong learning experience, and I had a long way to go before being able to offer my services to anyone without a bit more experience under my belt. However, using the information I learned from both schools, I continued my fly fishing journey and education and decided to open my own fly fishing school and guide service, Southern Brookies, the following year. In the years since my interest in fly fishing

ATTENDING GUIDE SCHOOL WITH REEL WOMEN

began, I had moved up the corporate ladder at Parsons Brinckerhoff and was still fully invested in the responsibilities these positions held. So this move into my fly fishing startup business would be a small, on-the-side endeavor.

One day on a float trip by myself, I drifted past two women in a canoe. We struck up a conversation, and I noticed they were fishing with conventional tackle. I began to tell them all about fly fishing and how they should give it a try. I explained that I was in the process of starting my own guide service and asked if they would be my guinea pigs on a complimentary float trip. They said yes! It would be my first trip, and I was nervously excited.

NONIE SANDERS AND PAULINE WILLIAMS, MY FIRST CLIENTS

Nonie and Pauline have since become dear friends, and I owe them a debt of gratitude for giving me some excellent feedback on my inaugural guiding experience. Just recently, I was sharing this story with a friend who had never taken a guided trip and was about to have her first experience floating with a guide on the White River in Arkansas. She suggested that I include a chapter in my book for newbies on what one should expect on a guided trip. She was feeling a little intimidated and thought a few tips might be of help. So thanks, Holly, for the suggestion. This chapter is just for you!

In this chapter you will learn not only what to expect but also some tips on how to get the most out of the trip.

What to Expect

The Cost and What's Included

A typical freshwater guided trip will run $275–$500, depending on whether you go for a partial day or a full day, and if you go on foot (known as a wade trip) or in a boat (known as a float trip). Half days typically are 4 hours, and a full day is 6–8 hours. The price can also vary depending on the area of the country where you are fishing.

It's always good to ask about the start and end times and the meetup and endpoints. For float trips, shuttles are typically included in the price. Most guides will list the items included in the trip on their website, but it's a good idea to go through this with them just in case anything has changed.

For full day trips, you can typically count on lunch and beverages being included in the cost of the trip. Be sure to let them know of any food allergies. Most are more than willing to accommodate special requests. Flies are typically included in the rate, but some outfitters have started charging for the flies used throughout the day. It's worth asking about it in advance so you aren't surprised by extra charges at the end of the trip.

If you are new to fly fishing, guides will often provide waders and boots at no additional cost or for a small fee. They will also supply the rod and reel if you haven't invested in equipment or if you are traveling and haven't brought your own gear. If you have your own gear, feel free to bring it along. If you are going on a float trip and have studs in your boots, be sure to ask your guide about this ahead of time. Most guides will not allow studded boots in the boat. They are slippery and can scratch the boat finish, so it's a good idea to check first.

Most times the trip rate doesn't include gratuity. It's common to tip 15%–20% if you are happy with the service. There are a number of great articles online regarding guide gratuity. I recommend doing a little research and coming up with your own standard for rewarding a guide. Keep in mind, if the fish aren't biting on a particular day, it's not the fault of the guide. The hard work goes in regardless of the number of fish brought to the net. In fact, slow bite days are very, very hardworking days. Don't be fooled into thinking that a guide is getting rich off of you. Once you take out the cost of gas, a good lunch, the shuttle payment, leaders, tippets, and flies, the guide walks away with much less than you would expect. For most guides, it isn't the money that brings us back. It's the passion for fly fishing, the time meeting new friends, and a day spent on the water that is the true paycheck.

LAUNCHING THE DRIFT BOAT ON TENNESSEE'S CANEY FORK RIVER

License and Regulations

Be sure to ask about anything else that will be needed, such as a fishing license or trout stamp. Many times the guide will ask for you to get your license ahead of the trip to save time and get you on the water as soon as possible. Most states offer online license purchases, which is very convenient. Just remember, each state has different fishing regulations such as the type of hooks or boots allowed. If you don't know what you don't know, ask your guide if there are any equipment, gear, or license regulations you need to know about prior to the trip. This should prevent any surprises and keep you out of hot water.

Pit Stops

Guys don't think about this much, but females sure do. What about bathrooms? Well, sometimes you get lucky, and you will find a portable toilet at the access point. Most times, you just have to find a tree. I have a few more details on this in Chapter 14 (page 129). Bottom line: Don't hesitate to tell the guide that you need a pit stop. They will probably take one too.

What to Wear

This will, of course, depend on the season. However, it's always a good idea to wear quick-dry clothing. You never know when you may take an unexpected spill in the water. For summer float trips where waders aren't needed, I typically suggest water shoes, shorts, a short-sleeved or sleeveless quick dry shirt, an overshirt in case of intense sunshine, and a jacket in case of rain. If you are wearing waders, you can still wear shorts, although leggings or quick-dry pants also feel comfortable. Don't forget a pair of thick socks to wear inside stocking-foot or boot-foot waders (see Chapter 7, page 65, for more

on waders). You will get a blister for sure if you go without them. See
Chapter 5 (page 47) for winter clothing ideas.

What to Bring

CONSIDER PACKING THE following items in case the guide doesn't
supply them or have extras. Many times it can make the trip much
more comfortable.

- Rain jacket
- Sunscreen
- Extra snack or water
- Toilet tissue
- Zip-top plastic bag or dry bag (for keys, wallet or camera)

- Hat
- Insect repellent
- Change of clothes
- Camera

With this information, you should have everything you need to
prepare for the trip. It's natural to be a little anxious the first time, but
once you hit the water, your attention will quickly move to the fishing.

Getting the Most
Out of the Investment

AS NOTED PREVIOUSLY, guided trips can be expensive, even if you
are splitting it with a friend. Given this, you should approach
the trip as an investment and mine every nugget of instruction and
knowledge you can while you have your guide captive. Here are a few
additional tips on approaching the trip once on the water:

CASTING INSTRUCTION

MOST GUIDES KNOW a thing or two about casting and will be happy to
give you a few tips. Ask your guide to watch your cast and give some
feedback. You may be able to get some added distance, tighten your
loop, or find ways to work out the dreaded tailing loop (see Glossary).

Techniques

If you spend most of your time nymph fishing and haven't tried any other technique, this is the perfect time to ask to try something new. I've been with clients who have never tried fishing a dropper, swinging a wet fly, or stripping a streamer. Guides will be happy to rig up your line and demonstrate their favorite techniques, explaining when and how they should be used.

Gear

One of the fun things about being a guide is collecting gear. We feel perfectly justified in buying several rods and reels because we need them to share with our clients. Your guided trip is the perfect time to experience the difference between casting a 3-weight vs. a 6-weight rod or a fast-action vs. a slow-action rod. Have you ever wondered about fishing sinking lines? This is the time to try it. Ask your guide to bring along an extra rod for you to use and make comparisons.

Access Points

If I go to a new river, I always hire a guide. I could spend my vacation trying to find spots on my own, or I could make the investment, hire a guide, and then go back later to the same spots. Locally, a guide can take you to spots on the river that you may not know about, even if you have fished on that very river for years. I recently had a successful day of fishing with two friends, and I took them to one of my favorite runs. They had double-digit hookups and were very excited! Both of them told me they had never fished that run and had always floated past this particular spot. They had no idea that the section held so many fish. Similar to this example, with a guide, you'll learn about cut banks, riffles, a sunken log, or a special run that always seems to hold fish. Make a mental note of these spots, and try them next time you are on your own. Catching fish helps to build confidence. If you know the fish are there, you often will fish more intently and with more patience.

Favorite Flies

Be sure to ask your guide about their favorite go-to flies. Remember these, or better yet, take a picture of the flies so you won't forget them. We all have our favorites and, most times, we don't mind sharing what they are when asked. It may not simply be the pattern but also how it's weighted, the color of the bead, the size, or the flash that makes all the difference in how effective the fly can be.

Other Fishing Waters

Ask your guide where they like to fish. We all have our home waters, but there are times when schedules, crowds, or muddy water makes us travel to other rivers. Middle Tennessee has an abundance of cold-water and warm-water fisheries. Your guide can share some of their favorites with you. You may be surprised to find you have some great water less than an hour's drive from where you live.

Fish Science

Have you ever wondered how to tell the difference between a rainbow, brown, or brook trout? Are you curious about spawning cycles or how temperature affects the way fish feed? Ask your guide. Many of us love to study up on anything fishy and can't wait to share our knowledge.

Guides want more than anything to put clients on fish, but on those days when the fishing is slow, it's a great time to look at the day as a teaching session. Soak up as much as you can while you are with your guide. Then you can put this education to use when you are out on your own. Remember, you are paying for the lessons that this day can provide, so get the most out of your investment.

Wintertime Fishing

Oneᴺᴱ ᴼᶠ ᵀᴴᴱ main things I wanted to do with my new business was to offer weekend schools. At the time, I didn't have a facility of my own, so I thought it would be exciting to offer an all-inclusive trip to the mountains. After securing a reservation on a large, multi-room cabin, I went on the hunt for a body of water where I could teach casting. Since it was late in the season, the campgrounds were closed. One of the camps had a great pond on site, and the owners were gracious enough to allow me to use it for the class since they were closed. Now all I needed were students. I advertised the first All Women's Beginner class online and, of course, the first two sign-ups were Nonie and Pauline. I had three other women sign up as well, so my first class was about to begin.

We carpooled to the little town of Townsend, Tennessee, on a Thursday afternoon and started class Friday morning. We spent the

SOUTHERN BROOKIES WINTERTIME FISHING SCHOOL STUDENTS

first half of the day inside the cabin learning about equipment, knots, and fly fishing terms. From there, we moved to the campground to begin the casting class. It was a cold day; in fact, it was spitting snow, with some accumulation predicted for the next day. This didn't stop us as we worked on learning the roll cast and basic cast. Partway through the class, a fellow approached to see what we were doing. As I told him about the class, I could see the excitement building in his eyes. He was with a local TV station and had been sent out to do a story at the grocery store about people stocking up in preparation for the snow. He said a bunch of women learning to fly fish was a much better story and asked if he could interview and film us. We all said yes! We finished filming and went back to casting. He promised it would air that evening on the news. After we returned to the cabin, we had a nice dinner and eagerly waited for the story. To our delight, the evening news opened and there we were! We were introduced as the "fly girls," followed by an exciting wintertime fishing story. We looked fabulous!

The next morning, we awoke to a winter wonderland. We don't get a lot of snow in Nashville, so we were beside ourselves. We had 3–4 inches and couldn't wait to get geared up in our waders to hit the river and put into action the skills learned the day before. If you haven't fished on a snowy day, you don't know what you are missing.

A number of fish were caught that day, but by far the most memorable was the beautiful rainbow trout that Nonie caught. She cast a black woolly bugger to the edge of an icy bluff and let the fly swing through the current. We all heard the cheer of "fish on" up and down the river. She had a smile I will never forget.

When folks see the picture of us on that icy day, many ask how we could stand the cold. For the most part, we dressed for it and were pretty toasty in our gear. As I've said many times, you don't need to pack your gear away just because it's winter! Many anglers use the winter months to tie flies in anticipation for the spring season, but if you can stand the cold, it's a great time to be on the water.

NONIE FIGHTING HER SMOKY MOUNTAIN RAINBOW

Cold-Weather Gear

HERE ARE A few tips that may help you as you venture out in search of wintertime trout:

• **BASE LAYER** As we all know, layering is key to staying warm in cold weather, both for your upper and lower body. You should stick with an inner moisture-wicking material as your base layer. The best materials are polyester, polypropylene, merino wool, silk, or other materials that wick moisture and dry quickly. The base layers will come in different weights for different weather conditions.

- Ultra lightweight: For mild to cool conditions; also referred to as microweight
- Lightweight: Cool to moderately cold conditions
- Midweight: Moderately cold to cold conditions
- Heavyweight: Cold, frigid, or blustery conditions

• **INSULATING LAYER** I like using fleece as a second layer for insulation. I also have a great fisherman's-weave wool sweater that a friend brought back to me from Ireland. It's one of my all-time favorite items. This layer acts as your primary source of warmth. You could also use a fleece vest or puff/down jacket in really cold weather.

• **OUTER OR SHELL LAYER** No matter how warm the wool sweater or fleece may feel to you, it won't help on cold, windy, or rainy days. If your insulating layer gets wet, you can get so cold that your day will most likely end early. Hypothermia isn't something to play around with; that's why this layer is so important. You can choose a waterproof or water-resistant material. Although a little pricey, a shell with Gore-Tex or Gore Windstopper material is best.

Keep in mind, layering doesn't mean you need to look like the Michelin Man. Incorrect layering will feel uncomfortable and binding. If you select the correct base, insulating, and shell layers, you will be warm while maintaining comfort and flexibility.

• **ACCESSORIES** Remember that most heat is lost from your head, so be sure to take a hat, preferably one that will cover your ears. A fleece neck warmer also works great when the wind is blowing, and it can be pulled up to cover your mouth and nose. Gloves, of course, are key to keeping warm. I like fingerless gloves with a mitten attachment. This allows me to remove the top mitten only, instead of removing the gloves, when changing flies or tying knots. On really cold days, I will slip disposable hand-warmer packs into my gloves and into the toes of my waders. This has extended my stay on the water many times.

• **CHANGE OF CLOTHES** It's a good idea to plan for the worst and pack a spare change of clothes that you can keep in the trunk of the car in case you take a spill. It's happened to me more than once. No matter how high you crank the heat in the car, a long drive home in wet clothes is miserable. I keep a small bag with an old pair of fleece pants, socks, and a fleece pullover in my car throughout the winter. I pack it once at the beginning of the season and leave it in the car until spring.

Other Considerations for Wintertime Fishing

• **PREPARE RIGS AHEAD OF TIME** The cold can make tying knots difficult. Fingers don't seem to move as quickly when they are cold, and working with very small flies can be difficult when your hands are shaking. One way to give yourself an advantage is to tie up several batches of your favorite tandem flies. This way, when changing flies, you will have only one knot to tie. The preassembled dropper rig can be wrapped around a piece of foam and stored in a small zip-top bag, or you can purchase boxes specifically made for this purpose.

• **MY FAVORITE WINTER FLIES** I spend most of my time during this season either nymphing or throwing a streamer, since hatches are limited. My three main go-to fly patterns in the winter are various colors of midge larva, woolly buggers, and bead-head pheasant tails.

• **SLOWER-MOVING FISH** The trout's metabolism slows down as the temperature drops, which means they aren't as active in cold weather and will chase down their food at a much slower pace. Consider this when fishing the woolly bugger or other streamers, and slow down the retrieval. Also look for deep, slow-moving water. The fish will be feeding in areas where they don't have to expend much energy.

TANDEM RIGS TIED AHEAD OF TIME AND STORED ON A FOAM LINE HOLDER

● **WINTER STOCKING** In addition to your primary trout waters, take a look at other bodies of water. In many locations across the country, agencies undertake a winter stocking program. Each year, in my home state, the Tennessee Wildlife Resource Agency releases trout during the winter months into creeks, rivers, and lakes that typically don't support trout, giving anglers many more opportunities to fish year-round.

Obviously, cold weather isn't loved by everyone, so the prime fishing areas won't be as crowded. In fact, you may have the water all to yourself. So bundle up and get out there. The thrill of catching trout will warm you up in no time.

THIS HEAVILY WEIGHTED BEAD-HEAD PHEASANT TAIL IS A FAVORITE WINTER FLY.

CHAPTER 6

Fly Fishing Clubs

AUGUST 2007 WAS the beginning of a milestone not only in my fly fishing journey but in my life overall. Nikki Mitchell and Cindy Denham were on my boat that morning as a result of winning a silent auction with the Hendersonville Fly Fishing Club. This was a Middle Tennessee club I donated my services to each year for their Christmas banquet. Nikki had contacted me earlier in the month to cash in on her winning auction item. It was a hot day when she and Cindy walked down the ramp at the Happy Hollow access point located on the Caney Fork River, just an hour east of Nashville, Tennessee.

DRIFT BOAT WITH ICE-COLD STARBUCKS WAITING FOR THE PASSENGERS

I usually have a thermos of hot coffee for guests as they arrive, but with the temperature already in the 80s that early morning, I opted for Starbucks Frappuccinos, which had been iced down in the cooler and were now just waiting for them to climb aboard. Nikki's first words to me when I reached into the cooler and pulled out the icy bottle was, "I just knew I would like you right away." That was the beginning of the best guide trip of my career for so many reasons.

During the course of the float trip with Nikki and Cindy, the discussion of fly fishing clubs, outings, and fishing partners moved into an idea that both Nikki and I shared for having an all-women's fly fishing club. Cindy was quick to announce that Nikki had created an entire folder full of ideas for beginning a women's group. At that very moment, we knew that we were destined to be in the boat together on that day, and we knew, with no doubt, something great was about to happen. Cindy even said she had goose bumps and that she had seen this kind of thing happen before with Nikki. Once Nikki had an idea in her head, it turned into a mental magnet, pulling all the pieces and parts into place at just the right time until the idea miraculously took form. Nikki referenced her faith and said, in these cases, she was simply following the path she was supposed to take. She said that, quite often, during times of new experiences, ideas, and adventures, she would find a white feather in the most unusual place and felt it was her sign that she was headed in the right direction. We all agreed that this was a white feather day for all of us.

As we continued our float that day, I went on to explain that I loved my association with Trout Unlimited and other clubs in the Middle Tennessee area. However, I had been dreaming of a club that would provide a non-intimidating environment, specifically focused on women, where an outing didn't necessarily mean 100% fishing all the time. Other activities could be included, and the club would still be taken seriously. Nikki and Cindy were both nodding in agreement and excitement. We spent a good share of the day discussing ideas on trips, possible group names, meeting locations, and themes. And just like that, the Music City Fly Girls club was born. We had our first meeting on October 18, 2007, with 15 excited and enthusiastic women in attendance, and we have been going strong ever since.

Whether you are a beginning fly fisher or an experienced angler, getting involved in a fly fishing club is a great way to discover new information and build friendships. Many clubs offer free or discounted casting and fly-tying instruction. It's also a great way to discover new places to fish both locally and in other states. The membership dues will vary depending on the club, but in every case, the investment is a fraction of the benefits that can be realized. If you don't have a club in your area, consider beginning one on your own. It's amazing how fly fishing goes beyond the limits of gender, age, and other demographics.

What to Consider When Beginning a New Group

CLUB MAKEUP

NOT ALL CLUBS have to be the same. Coed and gender-specific groups each have their place. It's really up to the group and what the purpose of the club is intended to be. Some areas may have a specific need for a club where couples can participate. In other instances, gender-specific clubs are needed to simplify traveling and shared lodging. In the case of the Music City Fly Girls, the Middle Tennessee area already had a number of coed clubs, so with the purpose and intent of the activities we had in mind, a gender-specific group made sense. Also, there's no reason why anyone can't belong to more than one club. Many Music City Fly Girls are members of one or more clubs based on the different outings and events each club offers. When considering the makeup, give some thought to the overall goals of the club.

LEADERSHIP

DURING ONE OF the Music City Fly Girls outings to the White River in Arkansas, we had the pleasure of meeting up with another fly fishing club from Nashville for dinner. It was a great night, swapping stories about the day. At one point, one of the guys asked the group how the Music City Fly Girls were led and managed. Rachel Whitney spoke up quickly and said with a smile, "Well, I can tell you what we don't have. We don't have a board, and we don't have boring board meetings." This was followed by the question, "Well, how do you get things done?" Rachel laughed and said, "We have a benevolent dictator. She tells us what the trips are, plans the trips, sets the prices, and establishes the meetings. We just pay our annual dues and show up. It works beautifully for us."

When the Music City Fly Girls were established, we all agreed on two main things: we wanted to keep it simple, and we absolutely wanted no drama! To that end, we abandoned the idea of having a board and officers and opted for a unique structure. As cofounders, Nikki and I did the planning together. Eventually, Nikki handed this task off to me because I loved planning. We felt it was important to have a member designated to handle the dues, so we have a treasurer, Cindy, who handles the account and records all transactions. This ensures transparency.

This approach works for us, but it takes someone who loves planning meetings and outings and who has a passion for the group. For others, a committee-based approach may make more sense. Individuals or small groups can take on pieces and parts to keep from overloading one individual. This doesn't have to be decided all at once and can evolve as the club starts to develop.

DUES

THE MUSIC CITY FLY GIRLS have had annual dues of $60 from the very beginning. This money is used to cover the meal for our guest speakers at the monthly meeting, to subsidize outings such as covering the cost of rental cars and groceries, and to pay for our website registration. We typically have a membership roster of 40 women, which equates to an annual income of $2,400. It's amazing how far this money goes to help in supplementing our various activities. This is how we have chosen to use the dues, and it works for our club. However, other clubs may have different ideas such as charitable giving, environmental activities, or scholarships. This should be discussed and determined with the membership while the club is in the formative stages.

MEETINGS

THE MUSIC FLY GIRLS meet on the third Thursday of every month. We have held meetings in homes, offices, and restaurants. For us, we have found that a restaurant is the most enticing and results in the largest attendance. As any Fly Girl will tell you, a little wine, in moderation, tends to enhance our monthly get-togethers. Currently, we are meeting at a local restaurant with a private room. Members place

THE MUSIC CITY FLY GIRLS CELEBRATING 10 YEARS

their orders at the register when they arrive. We have social hour from 6 until 7 p.m. and the program runs from 7 until 8 p.m.

Speakers include local fishing guides; representatives from various agencies, such as the Tennessee Wildlife Resource Agency, Army Corps of Engineers, and Tennessee Valley Authority; and other folks who can provide information on our local waters. We have meetings on topics such as gear, water safety, and fishing in foul weather conditions. Members have prepared and presented slide shows of trips they have taken that could potentially be a Fly Girl outing.

A favorite meeting that we include each year takes place in my backyard pool. This is our wader safety meeting, where members are invited to jump in the pool with their waders on and venture into the deep end. Knowing what to do if you happen to fall in the water

THE MUSIC CITY FLY GIRLS ON AN OUTING TO THE GREAT SMOKY MOUNTAINS

is extremely important. Experiencing this in a safe environment can help keep people from panicking. It also helps to expel the myth that you will drown if your waders fill with water. It's the panic, not the waders full of water, that can lead to drowning. Since fly fishing is a lifelong-learning activity, we never seem to have a shortage of topics to pull from for our next meeting.

OUTINGS

GROUP OUTINGS WILL be one of the biggest draws to any club. There are a number of benefits. Outings help to establish friendships, and the group seems to bond a little tighter with each trip. Traveling as a group can also provide a cost savings since we can split the cost for a large cabin or have multiple people per hotel room. Typically, each year we have four to five local trips, sometimes for the day and sometimes for a long weekend. We try to carpool to get the most out of the time together. We also have one or two destination trips each year to places like Montana, New Mexico, and Colorado. The excitement and anticipation leading up to these destination trips is almost as much fun as the trip itself!

GIVING BACK

ONE OF THE early ideas we discussed when forming the Music City Fly Girls was a way we could volunteer as a group and give back to the community. There are a number of areas where volunteers can make a big difference in the world. Stream cleanups, teaching kids to fish, and working with veterans are all wonderful activities. The Fly Girls chose to be involved with Casting for Recovery, a program that supports breast cancer survivors through the art of fly fishing. This has become a cornerstone of the club and is so important that I have dedicated an entire chapter to this effort of love. See Chapter 31 (page 269) for information on this organization.

COMMUNICATION

COMMUNICATION IS KEY to getting members engaged. The Music City Fly Girls have a number of tools for getting the word out. We use our website and the typical social media platforms—Facebook, Instagram, and Twitter. We also keep an email distribution list. Email can be useful, but it has its limitations. For example, group emails lead to inboxes flooded with unnecessary "replies to all." As a solution, we signed up for a free smartphone application called Team App, where members can sign up to receive chats, similar to text messages, from members. The app has the option of group or private messaging, a listing of all members and their contact information, and other useful features such as notifications of upcoming events and the ability to share photos. It's perfect for impromptu fishing outings or get-togethers.

This approach has worked for the Music City Fly Girls, as we are set up basically as a hobby. If you plan to take a more formalized approach, with an established board, then you may want to check the regulations in your state for filing taxes, along with the options for insurance. It may not be required, but it's a good idea to check. The main thing is to try to keep drama and conflict to a minimum. The friendships established and memories created will be endless and lifelong.

CHAPTER 7

Waders for All Situations

MUSIC CITY FLY GIRLS IN THEIR WADERS IN MONTANA

As COFOUNDERS OF the Music City Fly Girls, Nikki and I were always trying to come up with meaningful, educational topics for club meetings to keep the members interested. The majority of the members had never fly fished, so getting outfitted with waders was a big first step. One of our most memorable meetings featured several Music City Fly Girls as models, demonstrating different wader styles. One Fly Girl model at a time would come out with a different style of wader, and the pros and cons of each were described. We appropriately called the meeting, "Do These Waders Make My Butt Look Big?"

Since that meeting, almost 10 years ago, the fishing industry has come a long way in designing waders that actually fit women. The days of buying waders big enough to slide over your hips, resulting in a boot foot so large that it would need to be folded over the toes, are thankfully a thing of the past. However, there are still a number of factors to consider before making the investment.

Wet Wading

First off, let's start with the most basic and simplistic of all wading outfits: the wet wading approach. Wet wading means fishing with no waders whatsoever. You simply wear a pair of quick-dry shorts or pants and a pair of water shoes. This can be a refreshing way to fish on hot summer days. I typically wear Chaco sandals when I wade, but often, if the wading is a little more challenging, I'll wear wool socks under a neoprene wading sock and a wading boot. The wool sock keeps my feet from getting blisters, the wading sock keeps the rocks from getting in, and the wading boot helps protect my toes. There are a number of wading socks available on the market. You can't go wrong with Simms Guide Guard Socks (simmsfishing.com)or Patagonia Neoprene Socks with Gravel Guards (patagonia.com).

You need to make sure you know what is lurking in the water, however, before going this route. One time, while in the New York Catskills with my friend and former Wulff School director Floyd Franke, we were heading out to fish the Willowemoc Creek, a tributary of the Beaver Kill River. I had on my typical wet wading gear, and he asked, "Don't the lamprey eels bother you?" I responded, "What are those?" After he

pointed them out to me, it was the last time I wet waded in that area. Bottom line: Don't wet wade where there is a chance of an eel sucking on your leg. Yikes!

If wet wading is out of the question, then you will need to look at getting a pair of waders.

WET WADING IN QUICK-DRY
SHORTS AND CHACO SANDALS

There is a lot to consider, from style and quality to material, when selecting your perfect pair. You should think about where you will be fishing, the water conditions, and the weather to ensure you have what will give you the most comfort.

Materials

I T'S IMPORTANT TO select a wader material that matches your fishing conditions. You can choose from materials such as rubber, neoprene, canvas, and breathable materials like Gore-Tex.

If you know that the majority of the fishing you will be doing is in the dead of winter and in ice-cold conditions, then you may want to consider neoprene waders. Neoprene is the material used in wet suits. It is highly insulating with its thick material and, of course, it's waterproof. Neoprene waders come in a variety of thicknesses so you can fish all day in icy temperatures and be comfortable. However, slip these on in the heat of the summer, and you will be miserably hot.

If you plan to fish in a variety of weather conditions, then breathable waders are a better choice. In the winter, you can add layers under your waders, and in the summer, a pair of shorts underneath will work perfectly. Breathable materials such as Gore-Tex allow moisture to be wicked away, keeping you comfortable. They are typically very light and thus a great choice for traveling. Be prepared to pay a bit more for their comfort and convenience.

Rubber waders are heavy and bulky, but they are inexpensive and will last a long time because of the thick, tough material. If you are on a budget or just an occasional angler, this may be a consideration for you.

Canvas waders are similar to rubber in that they are tough. Depending on the thickness, they can be well insulated, adding warmth. Consider these if you anticipate fishing in areas where you could easily poke holes in your waders.

Wader Styles
STOCKING-FOOT CHEST WADERS

CHEST WADERS ARE full-body waders. These are ideal if you will be fishing deep sections of water above your waist. They can also keep you warmer in the winter since they cover more of your body. The feet are made of neoprene, which slips easily into a boot. Most waders these days have a built-in gravel guard, which slips over your boot and keeps rocks from slipping inside. If they aren't built in, you should purchase a gravel guard that slips around each leg of the wader near the ankle. There's nothing much worse than getting a rock inside your shoe midway through the day and having to waste precious fishing time while undressing to remove the stone.

FISHING WITH MY SISTER, CINDY, ON THE OBEY RIVER. LEFT: BOOT-FOOT WADERS. RIGHT: WAIST-HIGH WADERS.

I have tried a number of different waders through the years, and I have found Patagonia's Women's Spring River waders to be extremely comfortable. There is a felt-lined chest pocket for cold hands in the winter and a front waterproof, zippered pocket for quick access to your phone or camera. They are a little pricey but worth every penny.

Boot-Foot Chest Waders

These waders have all the features noted above, except that the boot is built in and does not separate from the wader. There are several advantages to having a built-in boot: they are easy to slip off and on; it's close to impossible for rocks or sand to get into your boot; and they keep your feet a bit warmer in the winter. However, they don't have as much support as the stocking-foot wader with a slip-over boot. If you plan to do a lot of hiking, then it's best to stay away from the boot-foot wader. You will have much more support with a boot that fits over the stocking foot and can be cinched up for a tight fit.

Waist-High Waders

This style of waders is great for shallow rivers and streams. When the summer temperatures soar, I find waist-highs are also much cooler. I have both Patagonia and Simms waist-high waders and love them both. I especially like the pockets on the Patagonia waders. They fit so nicely it's almost like having on a pair of pants. It's also much easier to maneuver and drop your drawers in waist-highs when nature calls, which is a big plus when you have to make that pit stop without losing too much fishing time.

Currently, waist-high waders designed specifically for women are not available. However, I have found that the Simms Freestone Wading Pants (simmsfishing.com) and Patagonia Gunnison Gorge Wading Pant (patagonia.com) fit pretty well in the smaller men's sizes. Another option is to check out the Women's Ultralight Convertible Wader by Orvis (orvis.com). The shoulder straps can be quickly released and adjusted to easily convert to waist-high waders.

Knee-High or Hip Waders

These are ideal for fishing from a kayak or canoe when you want to keep your feet dry but don't need a full wader. I'm a real fan of the Chota Hippies (chotaoutdoorgear.com). These can be adjusted to fit mid-shin, at the knee, or near your waist. They are a perfect setup for small streams where you are only fishing in knee-high water.

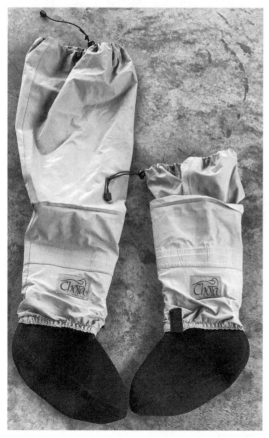

CHOTA HIPPIES ARE CONVERTIBLE FROM HIP-HIGH TO KNEE-HIGH.

FELT-SOLE WADING BOOT

Boots

BOOTS ALSO COME in a wide variety of boot and sole materials as well as cinch-up mechanisms. Again, the selection will be based on your fishing location, conditions, and personal preference. I have tried a number of different styles that have all served their purpose very well. Right now, I'm using the Simms Flyweight Wading Boot with rubber sole (simmsfishing.com). They have held up very well.

FELT SOLES

FELT-BOTTOM BOOTS WORK well on slick rocks, as they have tremendous gripping power. However, a number of states have outlawed their use because invasive species could become lodged in the felt and transferred from one stream to another. Be sure to check the state's regulations before fishing in water you aren't familiar with to avoid receiving a fine or, worse, contaminating the water.

Studs

Some wading boots have integrated studs that can be added and removed from rubber and felt soles. Some boots even have interchangeable soles. If you plan to be consistently wading in very slippery conditions where extra traction is critical, you may want to consider using studs. Stud-bottom boots help to get traction in mud and on rocks but wreak havoc in a drift boat. Show up with studs for a float trip, and most guides will have you remove them before entering their boot.

Rubber Soles

This tread doesn't hold as well as felt, but rubber-soled boots are a great all-around choice if wading in gravel or on small rocks or if you live in an area where felt is banned. They are perfect for hiking along the trail as you fish from spot to spot. They will also hold up longer than felt under heavy hiking situations. For me, the rubber-soled boot is the best choice of all.

When choosing the right wader, be sure to try them on while wearing a variety of types of clothing. If you will be fishing in the winter and will be purchasing breathable waders, try them on with fleece pants to be sure you have enough room. If you are buying stocking-foot waders, try on the boots with heavy socks. In cold weather, if you have tight boots that only accommodate thin socks, you will have miserably cold feet. It's more about comfort than anything, so keep that in mind while shopping for this important piece of gear.

CHAPTER 8

Not All Fly Lines Are Alike

WHILE I WAS growing up, my parents owned and operated a small travel business called Bristol Tours. Daddy, a full-time pastor, started the business as part of his ministry, and my sister and I were fortunate enough to travel all around the country and to many overseas locations. I think this experience, along with the trip-planning gene that I undoubtedly inherited from my dad, is responsible for one of my favorite aspects of the Music City Fly Girls. The Fly Girls take at least one big trip each year, along with a few outings within driving distance from Nashville. My love of trip planning has taken our club on some unique fly fishing trips. For example, our spring outing one year was to fish for peacock bass in the canals of Miami, Florida.

Nashville winters are fairly mild, but we do get our share of cold, blustery days. So when I mentioned a trip to Miami, a large group immediately signed up. We packed our gear, boarded the plane, and headed toward warmer weather. Upon arrival, we climbed into our

FLY GIRL SUSAN HENDERSON WITH HER FIRST PEACOCK BASS

enormous, black Suburban rental, cranked up the music, and headed off to find our Airbnb. We were all pleasantly surprised to have discovered the beautiful house in Coconut Grove that would be our home for the long weekend. The neighborhood is known for having wild peacocks roaming the streets. We loved seeing this unusual sight.

After unpacking, we headed out to have a Cuban coffee and a sandwich at a local café that Fly Girl Marjorie Rice had raved about. This was followed by a visit to a local fly shop to stock up on flies for the weekend. The fly shop owner recommended using large Clouser minnows in sizes 2 and 4. These flies were much larger and heavier than what we were used to using. We found out quickly the next day that our 5-weight fly lines and rods did not have the punch needed to get these wind-resistant, heavy flies launched into the canal with much grace. We managed to make it work, but the casts were awkward and tiring. We would have done much better with 7- or 8-weights. This was a lesson learned for our next outing. Although we were ill-equipped, we made it work and came away with some beautiful fish on that trip.

As mentioned earlier, I purchased my first outfit all at once—rod, reel, and fly line. The fly shop owner generously agreed to include the fly line at no cost since I was purchasing a rod and reel from his shop. I watched as he wound the backing onto the reel and then attached the bright-green fly line. All I knew about the fly line was that it was free (sort of) and it was green.

Since then, I've studied different fly line designs, and I find them to be truly fascinating. Maybe it's the engineer in me, but I love reading in depth about the tapers, densities, materials, and other key differences. If you geek out on this kind of thing too, then one of the best references I've discovered is a book called *Modern Fly Lines* by Bruce Richards. It's part of the *Lefty's Little Library of Fly Fishing* series. It is out of print, but you may be able to find a copy online or in a used-book store. For this chapter discussion, I'll just be focusing on the design basics and terminology you will need to know. I'll try not to overengineer it too much.

Fly lines come in various shapes and sizes, including those that float and those that sink. Knowing what fly line you need is really dependent on the type of fish you will be chasing, the flies you will be casting, and the fishing conditions.

Fly Line Design

TYPICAL FLY LINES are 90 feet long. The process that goes into the construction of this 90 feet is pretty complex but, in simplistic terms, most fly lines have a braided multifilament nylon or Dacron core coated with plastic.

As seen in the diagram on below, the 90-foot line is made up of a number of sections; each of these sections serves a specific purpose.

● **POINT** The line begins with a point, sometimes referred to as the tip. This is a very short, level (constant-diameter) section that can be considered a sacrificial part of the line. It is also where the leader attaches to the line. Its primary purpose is to give you room to change out leaders and to avoid cutting into the heart of the taper, thus damaging the line. Some manufacturers have started putting loops at the end of the lines to attach leaders with a loop-to-loop connection.

FLY LINE NOMENCLATURE

- **FRONT TAPER** After the point, the line begins to taper. This is known as the front taper and determines how gently or aggressively the fly will be presented.

- **BELLY** The front taper transitions to the belly, the thickest part of the line. This is where most of the energy is stored.

- **BACK TAPER** The belly section is followed by a back taper. This section transfers energy to the belly during the cast.

- **HEAD** The point, front taper, belly, and back taper are collectively known as the head.

- **RUNNING LINE** This is the long, thin, constant-diameter section, which is connected to the head of the line. This is the final section of the line and connects to the backing.

Whew, got all that? Who knew fly lines had so many parts? The line I have described and shown in the diagram on the opposite page is the popular weight-forward design, meaning most of the weight is in the front section of the line. Not all lines contain all of the sections noted above. Some designs have just a belly; some have a single taper and no running line. It's important to know these things because the existence and length of these pieces and parts will affect your casting. You will see how this plays out as we go through three basic designs: level, double taper, and weight forward.

Line Designs and Tapers

A s I mentioned earlier, the design you choose to use should be based on your fishing conditions, the fish you are after, and the flies you are using. There are three basic taper designs: level, double taper, and weight forward. Each line taper performs differently with its own unique characteristics, drawbacks, and benefits as you will see below.

Weight Forward (WF)

WEIGHT-FORWARD LINE DESIGN

WITH THIS LINE, the majority of the weight is concentrated in the front section of the fly line (the end that attaches to the leader). Manufacturers offer many varieties for different fishing conditions. The weight can be concentrated over a short distance (20 feet), giving a more powerful delivery, or over a longer distance (40 feet) giving a more delicate presentation. The remaining portion is a thin running line. The thin running line shoots easily through the guides with less friction, making this style better for distance casting than other designs.

One drawback is the limitation on how far you can roll cast or mend this line. You will need to ensure that the thick, or weighted, portion of the line is at or close to the tip of the rod before casting. It is almost impossible to control the thicker line with the thin running line. Even with the limitation on roll casting, however, this is the most versatile of all line designs.

Double Taper (DT)

DOUBLE-TAPER LINE DESIGN

THE TAPER ON the front end of this line is exactly the same as the taper on the back end. Connecting the two tapers is a long belly in the middle. Since the front and back are identical, the line can be reversed once the front end begins to wear out or becomes damaged. This is really like buying two lines for the price of one.

These lines are also very good for roll casting and for mending line. There will always be enough line weight to control the line that is outside of the rod tip. However, from the diagram above, you can see there is no thin running line, just one long belly. This makes the double taper less desirable for distance casting; if your casts will consistently be 50 feet or more, it's best to consider a weight-forward design.

LEVEL LINE (L)

THIS DESIGN IS just what the name suggests. It has a constant diameter throughout the length of the line. This is a poor line for casting because there is no taper to allow the energy traveling through the line to dissipate smoothly. If you ever cast a level line, you will see that it kicks back as the loop unrolls. There are a few specialty applications for using this line, such as Euro-style nymphing (casting a short distance and using mostly leader) and casting large bass flies for short distances, where stealth does not matter. A benefit of this line design is that the lines are relatively inexpensive. However, unless you are using them for one of the applications noted, I would stay away from them.

There are a number of variations to these three basic designs and tapers, such as long bellies, triangle tapers, and shooting tapers. The different lengths and taper rates of the forward and back tapers and the length of the belly will dictate how delicately or powerfully the fly will be presented. For example, if you know that you will be spending the day casting streamers, you may want a weight-forward line with a short front taper. The short taper will transfer more energy to the fly and make it easier to cast a heavier, wind-resistant fly throughout the day. As you begin to gain experience and start to experiment with different fly lines, I encourage you to explore, in even greater detail, these design variations.

Line Weights and Densities

As with the fly line tapers, selecting the line weight and density, meaning whether the line will float or sink, depends on the fishing conditions and the size of the fish you are pursuing.

LINE WEIGHT

FIRST, LET'S START with the line weight and how it works. The American Fly Fishing Trade Association (AFFTA) established a standard weighting system in the early 1960s, which set a weight in grains for the first 30 feet of a fly line. A number from 1 to 15 was assigned to the lines, with 1 being the lightest and 15 being the heaviest. This standard means that the weights are consistent among manufacturers within a set tolerance; if you buy a 6-weight line from one company and a 6-weight line from another, the first 30 feet of each line will be the same or within the accepted tolerance range.

LINE WEIGHT	GRAINS	TOLERABLE RANGE
1	60	54–66
2	80	74–86
3	100	94–106
4	120	114–126
5	140	134–146
6	160	152–168
7	185	177–193
8	210	202–218
9	240	230–250
10	280	270–290
11	330	318–342
12	380	368–392
13	450	435–465
14	500	485–515
15	550	535–565

Although there are exceptions, your fly line should be matched with a rod of the same weight to create a balanced outfit. Each fly rod has the weight labeled along the butt section of the rod. If a lighter or heavier line weight is used, the rod will not load or bend in the way it was designed to perform.

When fishing small spring creeks where the fish spook easily and lightweight dry flies will be used, a fly line in sizes 1-weight through 4-weight is ideal. The thin diameter will make minimal disturbance on the water and adds the necessary stealth required. However, when using larger, wind-resistant flies, such as bass bugs or large streamers, the larger lines are required to punch through the wind. In some cases, small, lightweight flies will be used for very large fish, which put up a strong fight. In this case, even though the line can easily cast the small fly, it won't hold up to the fight that's needed to land the fish, so the higher-weight line is necessary.

The listing below is a general guide in pairing the fly line with fish.

LINE WEIGHT	FISH
1–4	Small trout and bream
5–6	Trout, small bass, bream
7–8	Trout, bass, steelhead, bonefish, small salmon, redfish
9–10	Steelhead, salmon, permit, bonefish, bluefish, striped bass, redfish, small tarpon, muskie
11–13	Tarpon, king salmon, sharks
14–15	Marlin and sailfish

DENSITY

ANOTHER DESIGN ASPECT to consider in fly lines is density. Density is responsible for determining whether the line will float or sink. If you reach back in your memory to science class, you may recall the definition of density. If not, here is a refresher. Density is defined as mass per unit volume—in other words, how tightly matter is crammed together. It's important that you don't confuse weight with density. Weight bends the rod. Density determines if it floats or sinks. More on this in a minute.

Let's start by defining the general line-density types:

• **FLOATING LINES (F)** are the most popular and versatile. They perform as the name suggests, floating on top of the water. They float because the plastic coating is filled with hollow spheres, or air pockets, making the line less dense than water. These lines are used when fishing dry flies, weighted nymphs, and streamers at moderate depths. Floating lines will not sink unless you add weight to the leader or to the flies. This is the line most fly fishermen use and, if you can only select one line, it should be a floating line.

• **SINKING LINES (S)** are used when the fly needs to be fished much deeper. The lines sink because tungsten powder is used in the coating, making it more dense than water. The amount and placement of the tungsten powder within the coating determines how fast it will sink.

• **INTERMEDIATE LINES (I)** are a type of sinking line used when you want to fish under the surface of the water but not too deep. It sinks very slowly.

Recall from the AFFTA chart on page 82 that the first 30 feet of a fly line determines the weight of the line. So, if you weigh the first 30 feet of a 6-weight floating line and the first 30 feet of a 6-weight sinking line, they will be the same. This part may leave you scratching your head, but remember, weight and density are two different things. The difference in their buoyancy isn't based on how much they weigh; it's based on the density and how it relates to the density of water. Think of a 100-pound log and a 100-pound steel beam. Both weigh the same, but the log floats because its density is less than that of water, and steel sinks because it is much more dense.

Floating vs. Sinking Lines

Again, floating lines are the most common fly lines used. They are versatile in that you can fish dry flies when the fish are feeding on the surface, swing wet flies just under the surface, and weighted nymphs or streamers when the fish are holding close to the bottom. If you really need to get down deep, you can add some split shot (weight) to your leader to get the flies even deeper. However, there comes a point when even a heavy-weighted fly with split shot won't be able to get the fly down as deep and as quickly as needed. For example, if you are fishing in a river with a very fast current and simply try using a weighted streamer and floating line, the current will sweep the line and fly quickly downstream. The current moves so quickly there isn't time for the streamer to sink down to where the fish are holding. In this case, you will need some extra weight to make fishing the fast currents effective.

Systems for Fishing Deep

There are a number of line systems that can be used when fishing deep, fast currents or deep lakes. It boils down to personal preference and what you're comfortable casting. It's good to know how various line systems work so you can make an informed decision.

Sinking lines vary in their design. Some lines sink through the entire length of the line, and some at just the front end. They also vary in the speed at which they sink through the water column, known as ips, or inches per second. Let's take a look at these variations.

Sink Tips

With sink tip lines, only the front section will sink. The rest of the line will float. Since only a part of the line is sinking, the floating section can be used to adjust or mend the line to control the position or drift of the fly.

- **INTEGRATED SINK TIPS** You can purchase a fly line that has the sink tip built directly into the fly line, meaning the sinking portion transitions into the floating line with no knots or connecting points. These are the easiest to cast since the manufactured transitions keep you from having a hinge point. These lines are ideal when you know you will be fishing deep all day long. However, if you think you may spend time both dry fly fishing and fishing deep, then the multitip or sinking leaders system, described below, could be a better option.

- **MULTITIP LINE SYSTEM** You have the option to buy a floating line that comes with several sink tips with different sink rates so the tips can be switched out based on fishing conditions. The sink tips are attached using a loop-to-loop connection.

- **SINKING LEADERS** You can purchase just a single sink tip, known as a sinking leader, and add it to your floating line if you don't want to purchase a whole new line or setup. Many fly fishers will keep a sinking line in their pack just in case it's needed.

FULL SINK

As THE NAME implies, with a full-sink fly line, your entire fly line will sink. Most full-sink lines made today are density compensated, meaning the tip of the fly line, closest to the fly, will sink at the same rate as the midsection of the line. This means the fly line won't form a belly or sag once it's underwater. Instead, it will maintain a straight-line path. This is important so that you can stay completely connected with the fly and be able to feel the take. Full-sink lines are used in heavy, fast currents and lakes. They are difficult to cast, and it takes some practice. It's impossible to begin a cast with a lot of line outside of the rod tip. The line needs to be retrieved fully before recasting. Also, it's almost impossible to mend the line once the line sinks below the surface of the water. Even though they aren't as easy to cast as a floating line, they are very effective. The biggest advantage is that sinking lines will allow you to keep the fly deep in the feeding zone a bit longer as you retrieve the line.

Sink Rates

THE SINK RATE is simply how quickly your line will sink in the water. The line manufacturers use a rating system of ips, or inches per second, to help you know what to expect when fishing a particular sinking line. However, the labeling may vary between manufacturers. For example, one maker may label a line that sinks at 3 ips as a T3, while another labels the line as Di 3, Sink 3, or Type III. Read the specifications on the box to avoid the confusion. Keep in mind the reason you will be using the sinking line in the first place. It's to get the fly down where the fish are feeding. If you are in slower-moving water where the fish are holding in shallow water, you may need a line sinking at only 1 or 2 ips. If you are fishing a tailwater where the current is really rolling and you need the fly to sink quickly, then a rate of 5–6 ips will be necessary. If in doubt about which sink rate to use, ask the folks in your local fly shop or call the fly line manufacturer. I have found folks to be more than happy to provide information.

SINKING-LINE GRAIN WEIGHT

SINKING LINES MAY be numbered by grain weight instead of standard rod weight as typically found on floating lines. In most cases, the manufacturers will give a rod size recommendation to be used with particular lines. If in doubt, refer to the AFFTA chart on page 82 for grain weights. Keep in mind, the chart is a standard for determining line weights but doesn't provide a hard-and-fast rule for matching rod sizes. In many cases, you will find the grain weight of the sinking line to be higher than what is recommended in the chart for a balanced outfit. Yes, this is confusing, but remember, the chart is a suggested recommendation for a balanced outfit based on a typical angler's casting distance. For matching sinking-line grain weights to rod sizes, a typical rule of thumb is noted below:

ROD WEIGHT	GRAINS
5–6	150
6–7	200
7–8	250
8–9	300
9–10	350
11–12	450
12–13	500

Understanding the various tapers, weights, and densities can seem overwhelming to the beginning fly fisher. However, in time and with some patience, study, and time experimenting with the different designs, you will begin to understand the situations when these designs will improve your chances of a successful day on the river.

CHAPTER 9

Rod Selection

M Y SISTER, CINDY, once asked me, "How many rods do you really need?" My response: "One more than I already have!" You can get away with having just one rod, but if you begin to go after different species of fish, or you want to home in on your fishing conditions, then prepare to start on a rod-collection journey.

A few years ago, the Music City Fly Girls traveled to Montana for our highly anticipated trip of the year. We stayed in Ennis, Montana, at the Riverside Motel cabins, and fished a number of rivers in the area. Tight Line Adventures was a wonderful outfitter to work with, and Justin Hartman and his crew took great care of us on the rivers.

One of the Fly Girls, Alice Russell, suggested that we have breakfast at the Campfire Lodge. She said it was located right on the Madison River and we could fish there after breakfast. It was a brilliant idea, so we headed out first thing that day. It was a very chilly mid-September morning, so when we walked into the Campfire Lodge, the first thing I noticed was the wood-burning stove in the middle of the café making the place warm as toast. The owners had set up a long table for the group in front of a picture window looking out directly on the river.

MUSIC CITY FLY GIRLS AT THE CAMPFIRE LODGE

We sat down and were immediately greeted with a pot of hot coffee. Anyone who knows me can tell you that three of my favorite things in life are good coffee, a crackling fire, and a table with a view. Just as I was thinking it couldn't get any better, I looked over my right shoulder and saw a wonderfully stocked fly shop boasting a large Hardy dealer sign. I'm pretty sure my heart skipped a beat.

After a delicious, hearty breakfast, we wandered into the fly shop to look around. I was excited to see a Hardy Zenith 3-weight rod and a 4-weight rod for sale. Just as I was trying to come up with some good reasons for justifying the purchase, a voice behind me said, "I can make you a great package deal on those rods. It's the last two we have." The voice belonged to Bob Nakagawa, the fly shop manager. Bob has worked at the Campfire for the last several years and turned out to be one of the friendliest people I've ever met. He took several of us to the front lawn to cast a few rods. We were in fly gear heaven. I cast both Hardy rods, and they felt so good in my hand that I was having a difficult time deciding which to purchase. So, I ended up buying both. Bob matched up the rods with beautiful Hardy reels. A little decadent, I know, but I do have a fly fishing school, and students need to test out a variety of rods. At least, that was my justification on that day! Several other Fly Girls made rod and reel purchases, and we spent the rest of the morning with our new gear fishing on the Madison River, just steps away from the café. It was a perfectly satisfying morning for us all.

Fly Rod Makeup

BEFORE SELECTING A rod, you will need to consider what type of fishing you will be doing. Perhaps you are dreaming of the Florida Keys and landing a large tarpon but you live near the Smoky Mountains of Tennessee and will primarily be fishing small streams. If you purchase a rod that matches your Florida dream trip and use it in the mountains, it will not be very enjoyable. So, when choosing that first rod, think about the fishing conditions you will face most often. Let's take a look at the makeup of a fly rod and the various design options you will be faced with when making a purchase.

LINE-WEIGHT RATING OF THE FLY ROD

As STATED IN previous chapters, you want a fly rod that balances out the weight of the line you will be using. This is known as line-weight rating, or rod weight. If you are using a 5-weight line, you will need a 5-weight rod. Rods are designed to perform best when matched with the weight of the line being cast. If you over-line the rod, like placing an 8-weight line on a 3-weight rod, you could snap the rod in two; the rod wasn't designed to carry that much weight. Conversely, if you cast a 3-weight line on an 8-weight rod, you won't be able to tell a line is even being cast; the line is too light to bend the rod. The bend, or the loading of the rod, is what provides the energy to propel the line forward. Refer to the chart on page 82 to see the line weight that best matches the fish you are targeting, and match the rod to the line.

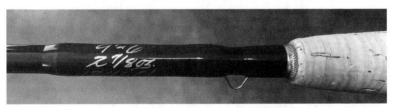

MARKINGS FOR THIS ROD INDICATE IT IS 9 FEET LONG, ACCOMMODATES A 6-WEIGHT LINE, AND HAS AN OVERALL ACTUAL ROD WEIGHT OF 2⅞ OUNCES.

The rod weight is written on the rod just above the rod grip, as shown in the photo above. Typically, the markings will show the rod weight, the length, and the weight of the rod itself in ounces. In this case, it is a 6-weight rod, it is 9 feet long, and it weighs 2⅞ ounces.

Over- and Under-Lining Your Rod

It is standard practice to balance the rod weight with the weight of the fly line. However, there are instances when over-lining or under-lining the rod could be appropriate. Manufacturers rate fly rods based on the average amount of line that will be cast in typical situations. In most cases, this distance is 30–40 feet. However, you aren't always going to be casting this average distance. Sometimes you may have much more line out of the rod tip than this, so rods are designed to handle lines a step or two above what is noted on the rod. *Note:* This information may help you understand the section on sinking-line grain weight and matching the correct rod to grain weight (see pages 86–87).

Let's look at fishing situations where over-lining would benefit you. Say you are fishing in a small stream, using a 4-weight line and matching 4-weight rod. The rod is designed to balance with the line at casts in the 30- to 40-foot range. In this stream however, the average cast will be less than 20 feet. After you subtract the length of the leader, only a short amount of fly line is outside of the rod tip, meaning there is very little weight to bend, or load, the rod. If you step up to a 5-weight line, the rod will load easier for these short casts.

In situations where you are making long casts on a very breezy day, dropping down a line size may be just the ticket. The lighter line will have a smaller diameter, making it less wind-resistant. You may be thinking that the lighter line won't load the rod as well, and this is true. However, if you carry an additional 10–15 feet outside of the rod tip on your cast, the additional weight will allow the rod to load properly.

Over-lining and under-lining are personal preferences, and fly fishing forums are filled with differing opinions. You should experiment with this concept and see if it helps when you are faced with conditions that could require some adjustments.

LENGTH

FLY RODS COME in a variety of lengths. A standard, all-around rod length is 9 feet, but there are situations where using a shorter or longer rod will be a benefit. Short rods, from less than 6 feet to 8 feet, are ideal for small streams with overhanging trees and obstacles. Rods in the 9- to 10-foot range are helpful when fishing larger bodies of water where you will be making longer casts. This also allows more line to be picked up off the water when mending the line. Longer rods, from 10.5 feet up to 15 feet, are typically used for specialty fishing situations such as European nymphing or big, open water.

ROD ACTION

ACTION IS THE term used to describe the profile of a rod as it bends under pressure applied at its tip. Consider a rod as having three main sections; the tip, the midsection, and the butt. A fast-action rod will bend at the tip, a medium-action rod will bend at the midsection, and a slow-action rod will bend closer to the butt. Each type has different characteristics and possible advantages based on fishing conditions. Once you begin to research the various actions, tapers, and degrees of stiffness, you can go down a rabbit hole quickly. As there are a number of differing opinions, my goal in this section is simply to give you a general idea of the options. Then, it's up to you to try out different rods and determine the action that best fits your casting style.

- **FAST ACTION** Fast-action rods are relatively stiff throughout the length of the rod, with most of the bend occurring in the tip section. You may hear the term *tip flex* when describing a fast-action rod. Fast-action rods are known for loading faster, producing tighter loops, and casting longer distances. These rods are often associated with saltwater fishing, as the characteristics noted can be of benefit when casting into the wind, casting long distances, and fighting bigger fish.

• **SLOW ACTION** A slow-action rod, sometimes known as soft-action or full-flex rod, is, as the latter term suggests, very flexible. Some might even describe it as feeling like a noodle. You can definitely feel the rod loading. It performs like a little shock absorber, soaking in some of the casting energy and protecting long, delicate tippets. It's best for short-distance casts and for presenting dry flies delicately to picky, easily spooked fish.

• **MEDIUM ACTION** Medium-action rods give the most versatility. They take the extremes of the fast-action and slow-action rods and meet in the middle. The rods can perform well while casting long distances but still provide enough flexibility to feel the rod as it loads. If you want one all-around fly rod that will get the job done on big rivers or small streams, go with a medium-action rod.

One final point related to rod action: In the end, it really depends on your casting style and what feels good in your hand. A good caster can make a fast-, medium-, or slow-action rod perform in any condition, but there are situations where a particular action will outperform its counterparts. Don't select a rod based on something you've read or what may be trending. It boils down to what feels the best when you are casting the rod.

Reel Seat

The reel seat is the section of the fly rod where the reel is mounted or attached. There are two types of screw-in reel seats, and each has threads running up and down the seat, with a locking nut. With up-locking reel seats, the locking nut screws toward the grip. With down-locking reel seats, the locking nut screws away from the grip. Most commercial-built fly rods have up-locking reel seats, but knowing others exist is good information for you to have as you expand your fly fishing knowledge. Some reel seat designs use slide rings

REEL SEAT WITH SLIDE RINGS ILLUSTRATING THE LOCATION OF THE REEL FEET AND END CAP.

instead of locking nut screws. This design uses pressure to keep the reel feet in place and attached to the rod. Typically, these are used with lighter-weight rods and reels.

Rod Butt

THE ROD BUTT is the bottom or thick section of the fly rod where the reel seat is attached. At the base of the rod is an end cap. Most trout rods have flat end caps; however, on rods used for larger fish, you will often find a fighting butt. This is a bulb-shaped cork located at the bottom of the rod, which helps to secure the rod against your waist while fighting the fish.

THE CORK FIGHTING BUTT AT THE END OF THE ROD IS COMMON ON SALTWATER RODS.

Materials

• **GRAPHITE** The most popular material for fly rods these days. The advantage is the light weight. When you are casting all day long, the weight will make a difference in how long you can keep going.

• **BAMBOO** It's quite a bit heavier than graphite, but many fly fishers love the feel of bamboo, from the cast of the line to the feel of the wiggling fish. They are typically classified as slow-action rods and are often associated with dry fly fishing because of the delicate presentations they are capable of making. The material dates back to the earliest fly rods, so bamboo rods are considered the "classic" fly rod.

• **FIBERGLASS** A little heavier than graphite but not by much. It is also durable and less expensive than graphite. Fiberglass, similar to bamboo, has a softer feel and is also ideal for delicate presentations.

Rod Sections

YOU CAN BUY single-piece or multiple-piece rods. With today's advanced rod construction, it's hard to tell the difference between them anymore. For me, I'll choose four- and five-piece rods every time. They will easily fit into the overhead bin when traveling, so they are a great advantage over a single- or two-piece rod.

Rod Cases

ONCE YOU DECIDE on a rod, be sure to protect that investment with a case. Frequently a rod case (for the rod and attached reel) or tube (for the rod only) is included, but if it's not, don't even think about taking a chance and trying to go without one. Chances are, you will accidentally throw a bag on top of the rod when loading up your car, close the tip in the door, or sit on it the first time out. Just bite the bullet and protect that investment. It will save you in the long run.

CHAPTER 10

Getting a Grip

FLOYD FRANKE TEACHING AT THE WULFF SCHOOL

ONE OF THE most fortunate experiences of my career has been my time at the Wulff School of Fly Fishing. As I mentioned in an earlier chapter, I attended the casting school in 2004. Later that year, I went back to attend the instructor school, where students would focus primarily on learning key teaching elements. At the time, Floyd Franke was the director. Sadly, he has since passed away, but his memory and legacy live on throughout the fly fishing community. Both Floyd and Joan Wulff gave excellent, in-depth lesson plans, hands-on how-tos, and other valuable insight into the art of fly casting instruction.

One of the most intense moments of the class was when each student was asked to teach a cast of their choosing, using what we had learned over the weekend. I chose to teach the roll cast. Both Joan and Floyd were observing the presentation, and then they critiqued the lesson and gave valuable feedback. It was quite nerve-wracking but one of the most educational experiences I could have asked for.

Following my time at instructor school, I was surprised to be offered an internship at the school, an opportunity that I couldn't have dreamed would ever come my way. This in turn led to a staff position, and I have been fortunate enough to be part of the team now for the past 15 years.

The Wulff School's class agenda is packed full, with many helpful sessions throughout the weekend. One of my favorite sessions is having the opportunity to test out different rods from various manufacturers in different weights and flexes and a variety of grip styles. The rod grips are important and should be selected based on the size of your hand, so trying them out is critical. One of the grips students always

CREATE THUMBPRINT

SAND THUMBPRINT DOWN

FINISHED DIY THUMB INDENTATION

comment on is the Wulff grip, designed by the Winston Rod Company. This grip is designed with a thumb impression so the thumb fits perfectly into the space. Winston will custom build the grips on any new rod model upon request.

If the idea of a thumb indentation interests you but you aren't in the market for a new rod, you can make one yourself. With a thin layer of shoe polish or ink on your thumb, grip the rod as you typically would, placing your thumbprint on the rod grip. Let dry. Wrap some sand paper around a coffee cup to create a rounded sanding surface, and gently sand the thumbprint until the shoe polish or ink has been sanded off. It's as simple as that!

Cork Grip Styles

I N ALL HONESTY, like most new fly fishermen, I didn't pay any attention or even notice that rod grips came in different styles, lengths, and circumferences. It wasn't until I had been fishing a few years that I realized this was the case. Different grips are designed for various reasons, so understanding these will help in selecting a design that fits your hand size and casting style. It can mean the difference between long, comfortable days of fishing, and those cut short because of aching forearm muscles and a cramping hand.

I have noted three of the common grips below.

• **FULL WELLS** The full wells grip is great for people with large hands, but if you have a smaller hand, it can become uncomfortable after a long day of casting. You will typically find this grip on rod weights 7 and above. Some fly fishers feel that it helps to give their thumb something to bump against when fighting a large fish and for making longer casts.

• **REVERSE HALF WELLS** The reverse half wells is the most versatile grip. It fits small to average-size hands, so both women and men

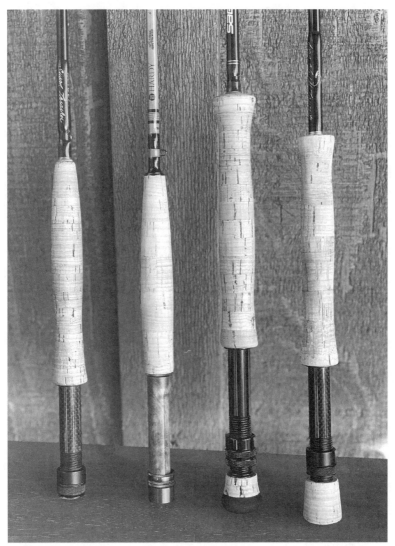

COMMON GRIP STYLES (LEFT TO RIGHT): REVERSE HALF WELLS, CIGAR, FULL WELLS, AND
FULL WELLS WITH THUMB GROOVE

can benefit from this style. The contours of the grip allow you to move
your hand to a position that best suits your hand. It's typically found
on rod weights 6 and below.

- **CIGAR** The cigar grip is an excellent grip for people with small hands. It's hard to find this grip on commercially available rods, but if you have a custom rod made, you can certainly request this grip.

As I've said before, it's important to cast a rod before purchasing. Making sure it fits nicely in your hand is critical in the selection of the perfect rod.

Holding the Rod

THE GRIP IS one of the foundations to a good cast. I have talked with beginners who mentioned a blister that had formed on their hand or complained of tired hand muscles at the end of the day. Both are due to an incorrect grip. You should never end a day of fishing with a blister or hand cramps. If you do, then you will need to reexamine the way you are holding the rod.

Your fly rod and line can be considered tools, and to maneuver them correctly and gain the most benefit, your hand must properly guide and direct them. Although there are a number of common ways to hold the rod, such as index finger on top for accuracy and the V-grip, I have found the thumb on top, as described below, to be most effective for me. Following the steps below will set you on the right path.

1. **Relax.** The death grip is a definite no-no if you want a smooth, pain-free cast. Think "soft hand," applying only enough pressure in the beginning to keep the rod from falling out of your hand. Feeling the cast is a large part of beautiful casting, so loosen up!

2. **Wrap gently.** Place your rod in the bend of your fingers, and gently wrap your fingers around the rod grip.

3. **Thumb pad on top.** The thumb should rest on the top of the rod grip, near the top of the cork, and should be slightly arched at the joint.

4. **Leave some space.** Leave a small amount of space between the rod grip and your thumb. This serves as leverage, allowing you to apply pressure with your thumb while pulling back with your fingers at the appropriate times.

5. **Heel on top.** Place the soft edge of the heel of your hand on the top of the rod grip. This will keep the rod from sitting too far into your hand.

Your personal casting style will dictate what is most comfortable for you regarding the grip style and how you hold the rod. No matter the style, one thing remains key, and that is to relax the hand and avoid the death grip.

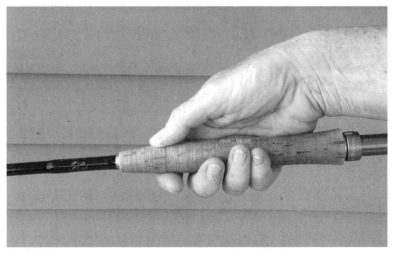

A PROPER ROD GRIP

Leader, Tippet, and Friends

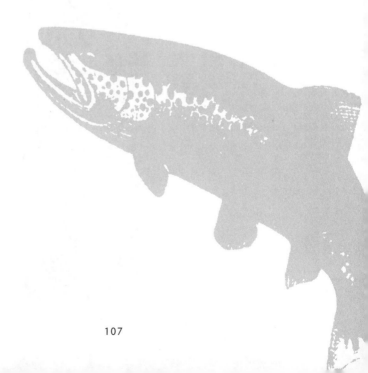

ONE OF OUR very first Music City Fly Girls outings was a weekend camping trip to Long Branch Campground on the Caney Fork River in Lancaster, Tennessee. Most of us had tents, but Nikki and Cindy brought their new vintage Shasta camper. The two of them had gone in together to purchase the cozy trailer, and this weekend was their maiden voyage. Nikki brought her sweet little rescued poodle, Lucy. The elderly dog was deaf and blind from years of mistreatment, but that dog received more love in the remaining short period of time she had with Nikki than most dogs receive in their lifetime. Lucy was outfitted in her cute fly fishing vest and fit right in with the rest of the appropriately outfitted group.

After a delicious breakfast of bacon, eggs, pancakes, and biscuits cooked in a cast iron Dutch oven over the fire, we gathered around to discuss the fishing day ahead. I gave the group a quick overview of equipment, must-know knots, and leader and tippet. For most of the women in attendance, this was the first time they had experienced a full weekend of fly fishing, so sitting around the campfire that morning and learning the difference between leader and tippet, the meaning

FLY GIRL ELAINE WOOD AT THE
PANCAKE GRIDDLE

ORIGINAL MUSIC CITY FLY GIRLS (LEFT TO RIGHT) NIKKI MITCHELL, NONIE SANDERS, CHRIS LOCKERT, AND MIDGE JONES

of 3X and 5X, and how to tie a surgeon's knot, was important conversation for us to have.

After a fun-filled day and with nets full of fish, we gathered around the fire once again that evening, enjoying a big bowl of Nikki's Lowcountry boil. This was one of her specialty dishes, chock-full of shrimp and potatoes. Nikki and I took a minute together to reflect on the past few months of brainstorming and planning for a women's club that had brought us to this point. As we looked around, we were so happy, amazed, and, yes, proud of this wonderful group we had brought together.

Now, back to that leader-and-tippet lesson I gave around the campfire. The leader is one of the most important pieces of gear in a fly fisher's vest. It serves as the invisible connection between the fly and the fly line. Leaders are designed to fit the fishing situation, and understanding their design and how the various lengths and tapers work together will help to make you a better fly fisher.

Here's how it works: energy is carried through the fly line and transferred to the leader. If you are fishing with heavy, wind-resistant flies, you need a short, stout leader to transfer enough energy through the leader to carry the weight of the fly and turn it over for a solid presentation. When the situation calls for stealth due to clear water, easily spooked trout, and small flies, then a long, fine leader is the best selection. The energy will dissipate over the length of the leader, resulting in a light and delicate presentation.

Manufactured knotless, tapered trout leaders start with a thick diameter where it attaches to the fly line. Then it tapers down to a level or constant-diameter section known as tippet. The level section is typically 24–36 inches. The "X" system is used in referencing the tippet diameter. As the X number increases, the diameter decreases. For example, a 7X leader is much finer than a 1X.

This form of measurement dates back to a time when fishers used the silk strands from caterpillars for their leaders. The strands were pulled through various-size extruders, or shavers, to provide uniform diameters. Pulling through once (1X) shaved the strand down to a set diameter. Pulling through twice (2X) reduced the diameter even more. An easy formula for calculating diameter size in thousandths of an inch is the Rule of 11. Subtract the X designation from 11. The difference is the tippet diameter in thousandths of an inch. For example: 11 − 3X = 8 thousandths, or a diameter of .008.

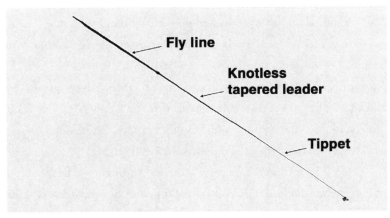

KNOTLESS LEADER, 3X DIAMETER

The appropriate tippet diameter for a certain fly size can be roughly calculated using the Rule of 4. Simply divide the size of the fly by 4. For example, a size 16 fly divided by 4 equals 4. So, the appropriate tippet size is a 4X. As you can see in the chart below, this is simply a rough guide to get you in the general ballpark.

TIPPET SIZE RELATIVE TO FLY SIZE			
TIPPET SIZE	DIAMETER	POUND TEST	FLY SIZE
0X	0.011	12	2–4
1X	0.010	10	4–8
2X	0.009	9	6–10
3X	0.008	7	10–14
4X	0.007	5	12–16
5X	0.006	4	14–18
6X	0.005	3	16–22
7X	0.004	2	18–24
8X	0.003	1.2	22–28

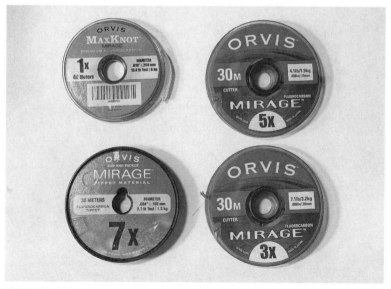

TIPPET SPOOLS IN 1X, 3X, 5X, AND 7X DIAMETERS

Keep in mind: the leader is tapered throughout its entire length so, as you change your fly and clip off pieces of the leader, the diameter will continue to change, and it will be difficult to determine the size. An economical way to make your leaders last as long as possible, and to always know the diameter, is by using tippet material. After you tie on your new leader, instead of tying your fly directly to the end of the leader, tie on a 12- to 15-inch length of tippet material. This helps to prolong the life of your leader and keeps you from cutting into the base leader each time you change your fly.

Tippet comes in various spool diameters and slips easily into your vest pocket. A typical approach is to purchase 7.5-foot 1X leaders and spools of 1X, 3X, 5X, and 7X tippet. Tie on tippet material as needed to the leader to pair with the fly you are using. To ensure a smooth taper, attach material in steps no greater than two. Using this approach, a leader-and-tippet design for a size 18 fly is shown below:

1. Start with a 7.5-foot 1X leader.

2. Add 12 inches of 3X tippet.

3. Add 15 inches of 5X tippet. The final section of tippet material should be a little longer to give additional elasticity.

Leader design is not an exact science, but the Rule of 11 and the Rule of 4 give general guidance in developing your own formulas for success and will undoubtedly make you a better angler.

CHAPTER 12

Knots to Know

A FEW SUMMERS AGO, during a Music City Fly Girls outing on the Caney Fork River, a group of us were floating the river in kayaks. At one point, I noticed that two of the Fly Girls, Deb and Susan, had fallen a little behind, so I slowed down to wait for them to catch up. Deb needed to add a new leader to her fly line and couldn't remember the nail knot, so she pulled over in her kayak and pulled up a "how to" site on her phone. Just like that, she was back in business.

Fortunately, these days we have a ready-made teacher built into our smartphones. There are a number of websites and apps that not only will graphically demonstrate how to tie a knot but, through animation, will walk you through the steps in slow motion. You never know when this might come in handy.

One of the things in fly fishing that you don't want to skimp on is your knot-tying ability. You really only need to know a few knots, but it's important to know them and practice them so they become second nature. I've heard the saying, "If you don't know the knot, tie a lot"— meaning just tie many knots however you can. This doesn't work in fly fishing. When I was first learning knots, I would slip two pieces of cord in my briefcase and practice anytime I was sitting still. The more you practice, the more nimble your fingers will become.

Given the fact that there are a number of websites available for learning the knots, I'll forgo explaining the detailed steps here and instead focus on outlining the knots you need to know and when they are used. I highly recommend the site animatedknots.com. The website is free to use. However, if you will be fishing in an area with no signal and want to reference a knot you may have forgotten, the Animated Knots app is available for download for a nominal fee. This way, you will have the reference with you even if you don't have internet access.

Attaching Fly Line to Leader

THERE ARE A number of ways to attach your leader to the fly line. I'll tell you about my two favorites; the loop-to-loop connection and the nail knot.

LOOP-TO-LOOP CONNECTION

Courtesy of Animated Knots (animatedknots.com)

MOST OF THE new fly lines come with a built-in loop at the end. This also holds true for most knotless, tapered leaders that you purchase. The simplest way to attach the two is by using the loop-to-loop connection. Technically, this isn't a knot but simply a way of interconnecting the two loops.

This connection is an easy way to attach the fly line and leader, but there is a catch. What if your fly line doesn't come with a built-in loop, or you have a leader minus the loop? I remember when I first started, the loop came off my fly line, and I had no idea how to reattach the leader, so in desperation, I used the "don't know the knot, tie a lot" approach. It wasn't pretty. If you don't have a backup plan, you will be stuck like I was. This is where the next knot comes to the rescue.

NAIL KNOT

Courtesy of Animated Knots (animatedknots.com)

To TIE THIS knot, you can use a hollow tube or a nail, but the easiest way is with a nail knot tool. There are several options out there; some double as nippers. Directions for use come in the package.

Keep in mind that the end of your fly line has a 6-inch section that can be used to tie on and replace the leader multiple times. However, after quite a few changes, you can use up all the tip, and then you will begin to cut into the front taper of the line, which is something you want to avoid. If you prefer using the loop-to-loop connection as opposed to the nail knot but don't want to cut too far into your fly line, there is a solution. You can attach a permanent butt section. This will require you to learn how to tie the perfection loop, but it's not that hard. I typically will use a 6-inch section of Amnesia (a kink-resistant monofilament leader material) to create this section. You attach the Amnesia to the fly line using the nail knot tool and then tie a perfection loop (described below) to the other end. This can remain attached for the life of your fly line. If for some reason it does need to be replaced, you'll still be cutting into your fly line. However, it will be fewer times than if you attach the leader directly to the fly line with each leader change.

A fly shop can set this up for you, but I'm of the opinion that you need to know how to do it yourself. A fly shop or other fly fisher may not be with you when you need to make the repair, so why take the chance? It doesn't take long to learn, so make it a goal to be independent and learn these knots.

PERFECTION LOOP

Courtesy of Animated Knots (animatedknots.com)

THIS KNOT IS needed if your leader doesn't come with a ready-made loop. Make the loop relatively small to keep a slim line form.

Attaching Tippet to Leader

THERE ARE TWO knots that I use when tying tippet to leader: the surgeon's knot and the blood knot. It's a good idea to learn both.

SURGEON'S KNOT

Courtesy of Animated Knots (animatedknots.com)

THE SURGEON'S KNOT is used to join two lines of equal or unequal diameter. This knot is easier to tie than the blood knot, but it does not have as slim a profile.

BLOOD KNOT

Courtesy of Animated Knots (animatedknots.com)

THE BLOOD KNOT is a very pretty knot with a slim profile. It connects two lines of similar size while maintaining the lines' original strength due to the multiple turns around the center. Be sure to make at least five turns.

Attaching the Fly

THE IMPROVED CLINCH knot is easy to tie with a little practice. You may have learned the clinch knot if you have done any conventional fishing.

Improved Clinch Knot

Courtesy of Animated Knots (animatedknots.com)

The additional step at the end is what makes this the "improved" clinch knot. This final step involves bringing the working end back through the loop, as shown in the graphic above. Otherwise, you will end up losing the fly and possibly the fish and end up with nothing but a pigtail at the end of your line

When you first start tying these knots, you may become frustrated and wonder how you will ever remember the steps once you are out on the water. Believe me, practicing will help. Try the little trick that I did with two pieces of cord or rope. While watching TV or sitting for a long period of time, practice over and over again. Your fingers will begin to move naturally and, before too long, you will be tying knots with ease.

CHAPTER 13

Wading Safety

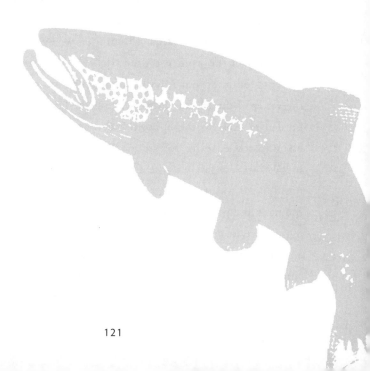

ONE OF OUR early Music City Fly Girl adventures was a fly fishing trip to Salt Lake City, Utah. We rented two large vehicles and drove to Heber City to fish on the Middle Provo River. As noted in an earlier chapter, I spent a year commuting for work between Nashville and Salt Lake City and spent many hours on the river during this wonderful time in my career. Because of this, I felt comfortable guiding my friends along this beautiful stretch of river.

Heber City is a small town less than an hour from Salt Lake City. During my solo trips to fish the river, I stumbled upon the Swiss Alps Inn, a family-owned motel that was clean and well priced for the frugal fly fisher. This, coupled with the great milk shakes at Dairy Keen a few steps away and a fabulous breakfast diner (Chick's Café) across the street, made it the perfect spot for us.

After we left the Salt Lake airport, we stopped in Park City at Trout Bum 2 for our fishing licenses and a few flies and then headed to the river. That's another great thing about living in Nashville. You can take a crack-of-dawn flight to Salt Lake and be on the river in time for a full afternoon of fishing. After a quick stop at the motel, we loaded into the cars and in less than 15 minutes, we were at the river.

Most of the women on the trip were used to the slow and easy currents found on our Middle Tennessee tailwaters, so the fast, rushing water of the Middle Provo was a little daunting. At one point, we needed to cross to the opposite side of the river to continue fishing our way downstream. To ease our angst, we formed a small chain and inched our way safely to the other side. This picture stands out in my mind like it was yesterday; a wonderful memory and a great lead-in to the next discussion on how to wade safely on the river.

I have been instructing beginners in fly fishing for many years, and there is always a slight bit of trepidation the first time a student slips on a pair of waders and steps into the water. As with any water sport, there are precautions that should be taken to reduce the risk of accidents. Being aware of the dangers and following a few simple, commonsense practices will keep you out of harm's way.

These are some of my tips for safety that are certain to keep your head above water.

Shuffle Your Feet

T RY TO AVOID picking up your feet. Don't blindly place one foot in front of the other, especially if you are unfamiliar with or cannot see the bottom of the river. Shuffling your feet will keep you steady and will help you to identify rocks and boulders before tripping over them.

Cross with a Buddy

D ON'T LET PRIDE stand in the way of getting to the other side and staying dry. When the water is moving fast, standing side by side with a buddy, with arms across each other's shoulders, will give added support to both of you.

MUSIC CITY FLY GIRLS CROSSING THE MIDDLE PROVO RIVER

Use a Wading Staff

A WADING STAFF CAN serve as a much needed support. It will allow you to check water depth, feel for rocks, and steady yourself in fast water when balance is critical. There are several options on the market today. A simple trekking pole or a fold-up model that attaches to your wading belt for convenience will do the trick. If you don't have a wading staff or forget yours at home, then find a nice, stout tree limb, and use it for crossing swift currents. I've done this a number of times, and it has helped to keep me dry. Check out the Simms wading staff (simmsfishing.com), which comes with a holster that attaches to your wading belt. Lately I have been using my net as a wading staff, reducing the amount of gear I need to carry. Fishpond's River Armor Edition nets (fishpondusa .com) are strong enough to support the weight. Fishpond also offers the Nomad End Cap, an accessory that can give you additional traction. The mid-length-size net works for my height (5'7"); however, it's best to try them out in a shop so you can be sure that the length fits you.

NONIE CROSSES A DEEP STRETCH OF WATER SUPPORTED BY HER WADING STAFF.

Cinch Your Wading Belt

K EEPING YOUR WADING belt cinched tightly around your waist will help to keep the water from rushing into your waders if you fall. I was fishing with my friend Susan Henderson on a small creek one winter when I reached out to pull on a branch stuck in the water that was impeding my cast. Without warning, it broke, sending me backward into the icy water. I had not tightened my belt, and in came the cold water like an early morning wake-up call. Fortunately, Susan let me borrow one of her jackets to help keep me warm, and we were able to continue fishing. If I had tightened the belt, I may have only had a wet shirtsleeve instead of being wet down to my toes.

Don't Panic

P EOPLE DROWN DUE to panic, not because of the myth that waders, when full of water, will pull you under. As I've stated, each summer I teach a safety class in my backyard swimming pool. During the class, students wade into the pool and allow their waders to fill with water. All are amazed to find that as they move into the deep

SAFE-WADING DEMONSTRATION IN THE POOL

end, they can actually float while treading water. If you do happen to fall in with waders on, get on your back with your feet pointed downstream. Keep an eye out for an area where you can backstroke yourself to shore, and then crawl out of the river. Once on shore, lie on your back, if possible, and allow the water to drain out from each leg. It will be much easier for you to stand up without the added weight of the water in your waders.

Consider a combination personal flotation device (PFD)/fishing vest. This is especially advised if you fish alone. Fly fishing vests with built in PFDs are available on the market today and are comfortable and stylish. And, of course, it's all about looking good!

Check the Schedule

CHECK THE GENERATION schedule if you are on a tailwater, and heed the warning that the schedule is subject to change. Most of the trout fishing in the Middle Tennessee area where I fish is on the tailwaters of the Caney Fork, Elk, Obey, or Duck River. Each of the rivers is controlled by the Corps of Engineers and/or the Tennessee Valley Authority. The generation schedule is posted daily and can be accessed using the following link: tva.com/river/lakeinfo.

There will be similar information in areas where you fish. Just check with the officials on your local waterways, and they can point you to the correct location for up-to-date information. Keep in mind that the schedules can change without warning, so you should be aware of your surroundings, paying close attention to any change in current. I make a point of picking out a spot at the edge of the river and watching for any change in elevation. This way, I can make my way to shore if I see a change, and I won't run the risk of being stranded on the wrong side of the river if the rising water catches me off guard.

Wear Quick-Dry Clothing

THIS IS A suggestion for comfort as well as safety. I have heard the saying "Cotton kills" numerous times from my good friend Lori Ridgeway, who works at one of my favorite Nashville outfitters, Cumberland Transit. Quick-dry material will keep you cooler in the summer months by wicking away moisture and, in the winter months, by helping to prevent hypothermia if you fall in the river.

Go with the Flow

WALK WITH THE current, angling downstream and across. Moving with the flow will help you with balance and will keep your legs from tiring out quickly due to fighting the current. Take one small shuffle step at a time. Why rush? Fishing isn't a race! Take your time and move at a pace that will allow you to catch your balance if you stumble.

These are basic, commonsense approaches to being in the water. If you can plan ahead, know your own personal strengths and limitations, and be aware of your surroundings, you should stay dry.

CHAPTER 14

When Nature Calls

F OR THE GUYS reading this book, you may want to skip over this chapter. It won't really apply to you, but if you want to know what we as women deal with, go ahead, keep reading.

I can't begin to count the number of times I have heard my female friends say, "Guys sure have it easy." When the urge hits, guys can just turn around almost anywhere. Problem solved. For us fly girls, not so easy. Hopefully, this chapter will give some helpful hints to the female anglers out there. And let's face it: we all want to know how to handle the dreaded potty break when fishing in remote areas away from all facilities except for a skinny pine tree.

This can be intimidating for women who haven't been brought up camping or hiking and enjoying daylong activities outdoors away from facilities. During my time as a guide, I've met a number of women who have never taken an outdoor potty break. I can understand how this can be intimidating, especially for a modest person.

CHARLEY WITH A BROWN TROUT FROM THE WHITE RIVER

Each year in October, the Music City Fly Girls take our annual trip to the White River in Arkansas. One member, Sheryl Mustain, has fished the area for years. She is an excellent fly fisher and freely shares her knowledge of the area with us. She also has a great network of friends and guides in the area, which always proves beneficial. Sheryl handles the logistics for this trip, which is a real treat for me. On these trips, I get to just tag along and fish.

The typical routine is to meet and have a hearty breakfast at Cracker Barrel, just outside of town, and carpool together. We also stop for a great Mexican food lunch at Casa Brava in Paragould and then make our way on to Dally's fly shop to pick up our licenses and, of course, do some shopping.

From there we head on to our rented, spacious cabin at Riverside Retreat in Norfork, Arkansas, located right on the White River. Chris and Carol, the owners, are the perfect hosts and always make us feel welcome and extra special.

We each have favorite guides for fishing the White River, so we make sure to get on their calendar way in advance of the trip. For the record, mine is Matt Millner with Rising River Guides. Then we count down the time until we can spend those fun-filled days floating the river. The trip is capped off

FISHING THE NORTH FORK OF THE WHITE RIVER BELOW THE DAM

by a wonderful dinner at PJ's Lodge, just a short distance from our cabin. It truly is one of the best events of the year.

On one particular trip, Jane and Phyllis (names changed to protect the innocent) had decided to be boat buddies. During the course of the day, one asked for a pit stop. If you've ever floated the White River, you probably know that it isn't that easy to find a good, secluded spot along the bank. I know many of you reading this can relate to what I'm about to say. When you ask for a stop, it means *now*, not in 10 minutes when the ideal spot is located. And sure enough, as their guide backed the drift boat in toward the bank, it was obvious that it would not be an ideal location for the task at hand. As Jane tells it, Phyllis climbed over the side of the boat, and Jane wondered where in the world she was headed. There were no trees to hide behind—just a flat gravel bar. Phyllis took a short walk away from the boat, turned around, paused for a couple of minutes, and then returned to the boat. Jane looked at Phyllis in amazement and mouthed the words "How did you do that?" Later on the ride home, they laughed about it as Phyllis shared the secret of her Lady J.

There are a number of female urination devices on the market today to make being outdoors a little easier. These are funnel-shaped devices which, bluntly stated, help women pee like men, while standing up and wearing pants, shorts, or waders. There are a wide range of styles, shapes, and sizes. Here are a few that the Fly Girls have tried.

● **LADY J** (biorelief.com) This little plastic device is small enough to fit easily in a wading vest or pack. The funnel shape fits close to the body, allowing the stream to be captured and directed away from you.

● **SHEWEE** (shewee.com) This device comes with an extender for directing the stream away from your body. It can be used with or without the extender and comes in a small, discreet package.

- **PSTYLE** (thepstyle.com) This device is a little larger than the other two, but it too will create a seal against the body. The shape is a little more open but easy to use with a little practice. Small cases are available for an additional cost. The case is so nice and discreet that one of our Fly Girls clips it to the outside of her pack.

What about tissue? I believe it's best to go without, simply for the environmental factor. However, if you must use toilet tissue, please consider a biodegradable paper that you can keep in your pack. You can also use a very thin panty liner, which will ensure dryness.

The use of these devices is obviously very personal, meaning the fit will be different for everyone. Each model is quite affordable, so you could try a few brands until you find the design that's best suited for you and your body. You want a device that works for you without leaking or splashing. My suggestion is to practice a few times at home before venturing out on your first wilderness experience. It takes a little practice, but it's so worth it.

THE SHEWEE EXTREME COMES IN 10 COLORS.

CHAPTER 15

Playing and Landing Fish

T HE FIRST MUSIC CITY FLY GIRLS adventure to fish the Middle Provo River was so successful, we decided to go again the next year. On our first full day of fishing, several of us were taking a break from a successful morning, sitting on the bank in the sun and just enjoying the sights and sounds of the river. The conversation was interrupted when someone spotted Elaine Wood, one of the founding members, standing in the middle of a nice run with her rod bent double. She gave a big shout. Yes, indeed, she had a fish on the line. In her excitement to bring the fish to the net, she dropped the rod and began hauling in line hand over fist. We all laughed until we thought our sides would split. After all the cheering and picture taking with her prize, we asked her why in the world she dropped her rod. She said matter-of-factly,

DAVE BRANDT DEMONSTRATING HOW TO HOOK AND SAFELY LAND A TROUT

"I didn't want him to get away!" Landing that fish was all Elaine had on her mind and, somehow, her method worked that day. However, there are easier ways to play and land a fish.

One of the weekend classes offered by the Wulff School of Fly Fishing is the Trout School. It's a beginning class covering all the basics of fly fishing. The final session on Sunday afternoon is on playing and landing fish. When Lee Wulff was alive and still teaching, this was his signature lecture. After he passed way, Dave Brandt, a longtime Wulff School instructor, excellent fisherman, and renowned fly tier, took over this lecture. He has always, without fail, been the one leading this lecture. The highlight is the final closing demonstration. The class takes a short walk to the stocked casting pond where he casts a dry fly to the edge of the water and then, hopefully, hooks and lands a trout using the techniques he has just described. One year, I had a call from Sheila Hassan, current Wulff School director, saying that Dave would not be at the school since he would be chasing brook trout in Labrador. She asked if I could lead the lecture. Terror suddenly gripped by heart. My mind was saying, "No way!" but I heard the words "Absolutely, no problem, happy to" coming out of my mouth.

We didn't have a recording of the lecture that I could study, so for the next two weeks I studied Floyd Franke's book on playing and landing fish. When Sunday finally arrived, Joan stopped by the school that morning and said, "I hear you will be leading the lecture this afternoon. I look forward to hearing it. You know this was Lee's lecture." Do you think I felt any pressure that afternoon as I stepped into the yard to begin teaching? You bet I did! After whispering a silent prayer, I began. Fortunately, I was able to cover all the topics I had rehearsed and seemed to keep everyone's attention. Now came the walk to the pond for the fish-catching piece. I remember praying, "Lord, let there be one dumb trout that falls for my fly on the first cast." And just like that, wham, there was a beautiful rainbow, sipping

WULFF SCHOOL INSTRUCTORS (LEFT TO RIGHT) MARK WILDE, DAVE BRANDT, SUSAN THRASHER, JOAN WULFF, SHEILA HASSAN, DENNIS CHARLEY

in my fly. He jumped out of the water twice, and then I pulled him into the bank and gently slipped the hook from his lip. The class graciously applauded, and we headed back into the school for our final class wrap-up. I let out a huge sigh of relief, and then some of the best words were whispered into my ear. Joan leaned over, and with a squeeze of my shoulder said, "Nicely done." That afternoon is seared into my memory forever.

Here are a few tips from that lecture that may help in landing the big one.

Setting the Hook

SEEING A FISH taking your fly causes a rush of adrenaline. However, to properly set the hook, you have to control that excitement, as hard as it may be at times. I've worked with beginning fly fishers, trying to set the stage in preparation for this before the first fly is even cast. However, most of the time, the excitement takes over, and the hook is set with such force I'm certain the lips were ripped right off the fish. It takes some practice to develop that soft-touch muscle memory. Basically, all it takes is tension in the line, and the fish will hook themselves.

The amount of force applied is similar to making a cast. If you can imagine gently picking the line up off the water as if you are making a backcast, then you will have dialed into the force that's needed.

Rod Tip Up

As I'M WRITING this, I'm picturing an Orvis logo with a fly fisherman on his tiptoes, rod held high above his head, with a rainbow-shaped bend in the rod. If you are ever out fishing with a guide, you will hear a shout once you hook the fish: "Rod tip up!" This is so the flexible end of the rod can be used as a shock absorber and cushion the pull and sudden movements of the fish. The angle of the rod that is most efficient is perpendicular to the fish. If there is too great an angle, meaning the rod is too far back, you will lose the spring or absorbency of the rod. If the angle is too short, you may have some pulling power but again not the absorbency. The kiss-of-death position when trying to land a fish is a straight rod pointed directly down toward the fish. With almost guaranteed certainty, if the rod is pointed straight downward, the fish will be gone.

All that said, there are times when the "rod tip up" rule needs to be relaxed. If the fish is panicking, oftentimes it will leap from the water, trying to shake the hook. There is a possibility that the fish will land on the leader on its return to the water. In this case, lowering the rod tip will add a little slack to the line, helping to keep the leader from breaking.

Keep the Pressure On

Okay, now that you have hooked the fish, what's next? The pressure will vary based on what the fish is doing. You will want to apply the lightest pressure at the beginning of the fight. Once hooked, the fish will be panicking and will begin to run. When this happens, let the fish run. In most cases you won't need to use the drag on your reel unless it's a very large fish. If you do need the drag, it will be set so the fish can easily pull line off the reel. Without a drag, you can use your palm to slow down the speed of the reel. If you have a pile of line at your feet, and you are controlling the line with your hand, then let the fish pull line from your fingers. You do not want to hold on for dear life and muscle the fish to the surface when he is in this dynamic state. This is where the finesse of fly fishing comes in. Playing the fish is like a dance. You each give a little going back and forth. You will be able to tell when the fish is starting to get tired. In some cases, the fish will hug the bottom or start to sulk. Once it is in this static state, it's OK to apply pressure to the fish. You can change the plane of the rod to turn the fish's head from one side to the other. Let the rod do its job to turn the fish. It's a powerful, shock-absorbing tool, so this is the time to use it. As you begin to slowly bring the fish in, it may still have some energy and begin to run again. If this happens, let it go. Depending on the size of the fish, this may happen a few times. When you start to see it tire, you will know when it's time to bring it all the way in.

Slack in the Line

A S A RULE, you want to maintain a connection to the fish and try to keep from giving slack while fighting the fish. However, there are times when slack can be a benefit. Here is a real-life example: During the weekend classes at the Wulff School, the instructors have an opportunity on Saturday evening after dinner to slip off to the river for a little fishing. The Beaverkill River near the school is private water, and only two river passes are available. The instructors take turns with the passes, and on this particular evening, Sheila Hassan and I were the lucky ones, scoring the passes. We ventured out into

THE COVETED BEAVERKILL RIVER
FISHING PASS

the stream, and within a few short minutes, I hooked a really great fish—that took off downstream! I knew I would be putting too much pressure on the fish if I held tight to the rod, and there wasn't room on the bank to chase after it. Even worse, I could see a fast current ahead leading to a logjam. If I let the fish run too far, it would be over. So, putting into practice what I had been taught, I stripped line off the reel quickly and delivered a roll cast downstream ahead of the fish, putting slack in the line. The current caught the slack-line belly of the fly line and began to pull the fish downstream. This fooled it into thinking I had changed positions and was below it. Amazingly, it worked! The fish turned and begin swimming back upstream, away from the pull and toward me. As it began to tire, I called to Sheila to bring the camera. The fish was definitely picture worthy, but we had left the camera in the car. I let out a bunch of slack line and left the rod on the bank while running back to the car for the camera. Since the fish was in a static state and sulking on the bottom, I was able to leave the slack in the line with no problem. Once back, I retrieved the fish, took the photo, and released him to be caught another day.

Landing the Fish

THE SAFEST AND most effective way to land the fish is with a landing net. When stripping in the line to bring the fish close, be careful that the leader doesn't come into the rod tip. You will want to keep a portion of the fly line outside the tip for added strength. Simply raise the rod tip up with one hand and use the net hand to guide the fish into the net headfirst. You never want to try and load him in tailfirst. This can be a disaster, which reminds me of one time on the Ruby River in Montana with my friend Top. Top isn't a fly fisher but loves the water and quite often will join me on the water searching for rocks or fossils along the bank. On this particular day, I hooked my best fish of the afternoon. I had left my net on the bank, so I called for Top to help me land the fish. Since she wasn't a fly fisher, she didn't know the headfirst rule, and in my excitement I failed to give her any instruction. To my horror, she began chasing the fish around in circles and trying to land the fish tailfirst. Needless to say, this resulted in a lost fish and a few grumbles on my part that were not received very well. Of course, this was all my fault because I had given little to no instruction. We laugh about this now, but at the time it wasn't that funny. Bottom line, bring the fish in headfirst.

The Release

GETTING FISH SAFELY back into the water unharmed should be a top priority. Ideally, fish should be revived in a relatively slow current. Releasing fish in a strong current when they are already tired will not bode well for their survival. Never move fish back and forth in the water. This can cause harm since they need water moving over their gills to extract oxygen. Water flowing the opposite way will not properly draw the oxygen needed. Release your fish with its head facing into the current. Once revived, they will swim from your hand on their own.

CHAPTER 16

Fish Identification

Fly fishing can be enjoyed in solitude or with a group. Both have their advantages. I personally find that when fishing alone, my thoughts travel to a hundred different places, brainstorming new ideas and activities and reliving past memories. One day, when I hooked and landed my largest rainbow trout of the season, my mind broke into the hymn "Count Your Blessings." This brought back a flood of memories from times when my sister and I would visit my grandparents during the summer in Mobile, Alabama. My Granddaddy Ennis was a pastor, and I could picture him leading the singing, standing on the platform of the Mobile Revival Center, belting out with all his heart, "Count your many blessings, name them one by one."

The phrase "name them one by one" led right into another wonderful memory. During that first float trip with Nikki and Cindy, as we floated down the Caney Fork River on that hot August day, we were fortunate to be hooking into a good number of fish. All of the fish we caught were trout—rainbows and browns—and Nikki had a name ready for each one. She would lift the fish from the net, quickly give them a name, and then release them. At one point, she and Cindy both asked how one could tell the difference between the various trout, and I was excited to share the details.

The three most common cold-water fish for fly fishers are rainbow, brown, and brook trout. There are a number of differences between these three, and sometimes those can be subtle, but you can always tell them apart, if you know what to watch for. See insert for a color comparison.

Brook Trout

Though commonly called trout, brook trout are actually part of the char family. They have a number of distinguishing features that make them easy to identify. This is a beautifully colored fish with

BROOK TROUT FROM A SMALL COLORADO ALPINE LAKE. NOTE THE WHITE EDGES ON THE FINS.

dark olive-colored sides that are scattered with red spots encircled by blue halos. On the back, you will see dark yellow or mushroom-colored squiggly lines. The feature that is most recognizable is found along the leading edges of the pectoral, pelvic, and anal fins. The fins' edges are tipped in white and stand out clearly against the darker background. The brook trout's tail fin is less forked than that of other trout; thus, the fish is sometimes called a squaretail.

During the spawn, as with all trout, the female digs out a shallow depression, known as a redd, where she deposits her eggs. Once the eggs are fertilized by the male, the female covers them with gravel, and the young fish hatch the following spring. The mature trout's features become easily distinguishable. Mature males develop a kype, or large hooked lower jaw, which becomes more pronounced as they age. As the female fattens with eggs, her head can appear more narrow and slender. Another distinguishing feature is the difference in the anal fin. In females, it curves inward toward the body (concave), whereas the male's fin curves outward away from the body (convex). Brook trout spawn in the fall, and their coloring during this time is brilliant, with vibrant red or orange bellies.

Brook trout require clean, clear, and cold water that is also well oxygenated. The ideal and preferred temperature for brook trout is from 57°F–61°F. Water temperatures in the high 70s or above are lethal to the trout.

The brook trout diet consists of aquatic insects, terrestrials, crustaceans, small fish, and crayfish. The feeding temperature is between 45°F and 65°F. At lower or higher temperatures, the fish become lethargic and feeding is limited.

Brown Trout

THE BROWN TROUT is a favorite of fly fishers for a number of reasons. It is known to be a more difficult fish to catch than the rainbow and brook trout, so the challenge in pursuing this fish is a big part of the allure. Browns also live longer and, therefore, tend to grow larger. The typical life expectancy of a brown trout is 5–7 years; however, some live much longer, up to 15 years.

Brown trout will certainly eat a fly, but it must be presented with precision. They are particularly cautious and hang out along undercut banks in deep pools and under heavy brush or fallen logs. These areas can be difficult to reach with a fly, which increases the challenge. They are aggressive, and it's exciting to hook, play, and land these fighters.

The brown trout has a number of distinct features. It is typically golden brown with large brown or black spots, and occasional red spots, on its sides. The belly is a lighter yellow. The spots are often surrounded by light-colored halos. The tail typically does not have

SUSAN AND GOOD FRIEND/PROFESSIONAL GUIDE DAVID KNAPP SHOW OFF RAINBOW (LEFT) AND BROWN TROUT (RIGHT). *Photographed by David Perry*

any spots; if any exist, they are very light in color and are only on the top half of the tail.

As with all trout, the brown requires clean, cold, well-oxygenated water. Brown trout can stand slightly warmer water than brook trout. They will survive in water that is consistently over 72°F and can withstand frigid temperatures, but their ideal temperature for growth is between 55°F and 65°F.

Brown trout feed on aquatic insects, terrestrials, and crustaceans, but as they begin to grow, they become piscivorous, meaning they began to feed on other fish. This ravenous feeding starts once they reach 12–14 inches. At this point, they actively pursue minnows, shad, and sculpin as well as mice and frogs. This is why flies such as Clouser minnows and other meaty streamer patterns can be productive in catching large trout. Brown trout are also known to be nocturnal feeders. The big monster browns come out from the cut banks at night to hunt their prey, particularly in the summer months. For the angler willing to venture out after dark, this is the time when chances improve for landing those enormous browns we all dream about.

Rainbow Trout

THE RAINBOW TROUT, a member of the salmon family, is one of the most popular and well known of the game fish. They are successfully bred in hatcheries and populate streams, rivers, and lakes around the world. Rainbow trout exist on every continent except Antarctica.

The coloring of a rainbow trout is a unique combination of greens, blues, and yellows. They are darker along the upper part of the body, with the color softening along the sides and becoming off-white or silver along the belly. They are covered with dark spots from head to tail. The rainbow trout's most distinctive feature is the pinkish-red band along its side.

Rainbow trout spawn during the late winter and early spring months of February–April. The distinctive pink band becomes more brilliant around the time of spawning.

Rainbow trout feed on the surface more frequently than brown and brook trout. They also prefer faster water, riffles, and open runs and are known to be more acrobatic, leaping from the water multiple times when caught. They prefer temperatures below 70°F, with their ideal temperature ranging from 55°F to 65°F.

The rainbow trout's diet consists of larval, pupal, and adult insects, such as midges, mayflies, caddis flies, and stone flies. They also have a fondness for fish eggs and small fish; however, they are not as piscivorous or aggressive as brown trout.

Fly fishers in areas of the country with rivers flowing out to sea or into large lakes are lucky enough to fish for migratory rainbow trout. Although they are the same species, these fish have an exciting and very different lifestyle, leaving freshwater rivers and moving to the ocean or expansive lakes, where they become voracious feeders and grow to be quite large. These migrating adults are known as steelhead trout because they turn silver in color. They can spend years in the ocean or lake, returning to freshwater rivers to spawn.

I believe being able to identify the species of fish that take your fly adds to the enjoyment of the overall fishing experience. Once you recognize and learn their distinct features, you will be able to comment confidently to your fishing partner as you bring the fish to the net, "Oh, another brownie. Just beautiful" or "I love these brookies, hand painted by God" or "Wow, look at that rainbow leap from the water. That brilliant red stripe is amazing!"

CHAPTER 17

Etiquette on the River

F LY FISHING CAN be described in many different ways. Some of my favorites are tranquil, serene, quiet, and calming. However, there are times when we can let the actions of others ruin a perfectly good day of fishing if we aren't careful.

Many times I have been in situations where I've thought, "Did that really just happen?" Once I had a fly fisher cast so close to me that he became tangled in my line. I've had kayakers run mindlessly into my drift boat while not paying attention to what they were doing.

On one trip with my sister, Cindy, and my nephew, Cody, we were having a wonderful day wade fishing in a beautiful spot on the river. A fisherman in a johnboat with a large, noisy motor came upriver at a high rate of speed, throwing an enormous wake and almost swamping our waders. I thought it was so rude that I couldn't help shouting out in anger to let him know that I didn't appreciate his behavior. At the time, I felt justified and empowered by speaking my mind. However, after my anger cooled, I was left with an empty feeling, and I was truly embarrassed by my actions. It wasn't the example I wanted to set for my nephew, and it certainly isn't what fly fishing is all about. I thought, "Where is the peacefulness in this?" That very day I decided to make a change. I would do everything possible to approach my fishing trips with an attitude of thankfulness, patience, and humility. I now carry a printed scripture verse in my boat bag as a reminder:

> *"Get rid of all bitterness, rage and anger, brawling and slander, along with every form of malice. Be kind and compassionate to one another, forgiving each other, just as Christ forgave you."*   —Ephesians 4:31–32

Even now, however, I'm far from perfect. I'll see someone on the river acting in a way that I think is wrong and immediately put on my "Citizen's Arrest! Citizen's Arrest!" attitude, like Gomer Pyle in an old

CHARLEY HALE AND ANGELA MILLET, THE CREEK BANDITS

Andy Griffith episode. My goal is to be more tenderhearted and forgiving for sure, but I have a ways to go.

What I've started to realize is that most people aren't out to cause you misery. They simply don't know about river etiquette. Yes, there are those people who for some reason don't care. However, I believe they are the exceptions, and most are just not aware. As fly fishers, we should all do our part to understand what it means to have good river etiquette. It's mostly common sense and following the Golden Rule. But in some cases, it's also about the local regulations.

Related to this is one of the funniest Music City Fly Girl memories I have. On one of our annual White River trips, we decided to spend one day wade fishing. It was a beautiful October morning when we stepped into the river below Norfork Dam. Although we were all happy to be in the water, there was a lot more fishing going on than catching. So Charley and Angie decided to break away from the group in search of some different water. About half an hour later, we started getting text messages from them. They had found fish, and not just any fish. They were catching one large trout after another and told us to pack up and head their way in a hurry. In the meantime, Sheryl had walked back to the parking lot and decided to take a look at Dry Run

Creek, located adjacent to the parking area. Dry Run Creek is located next to the Norfork Hatchery. It is a special creek set aside as a catch-and-release stream for disabled anglers and kids under 16 years of age.

As Sheryl walked closer to the creek, she began to hear loud cheers from voices she recognized. As she feared, she saw Angie and Charley, high-fiving over an enormous trout they had just landed. Somehow, they missed the posted sign detailing the regulations. Sheryl very firmly chastised them, and they immediately left the water. On one hand, they were embarrassed by the mistake, but on the other, they were still feeling the excitement over landing a handful of giant trout. We still give them a hard time about this faux pas.

Here are a few tips to remember on practicing good etiquette on the river.

Know the Regulations

IF YOU ARE fishing in a new location, be sure to understand the local fishing regulations. Local fly shops can help you with this if you don't have a copy of the printed materials. In some cases, there could be areas closed due to spawning, a requirement for using barbless hooks, or even age-restricted areas, as our Fly Girl bandits learned the hard way. Not only will this keep you from getting fined but, most important, it could also help keep the fish from being harmed.

Keep a Little Distance

FLY FISHING OBVIOUSLY is not like fishing with conventional tackle. You need enough space to cast so you don't hook other anglers. You will also be drifting your fly downstream, so give enough space to avoid tangling lines with other anglers. It's really best to find another run or pool if someone is already fishing in a certain spot. There's plenty of river to go around.

Share a Little

THERE ARE PLACES on the river that are ideal spots for fish to congregate. These are great finds, and it's a blast to pull out one fish after another in these honey holes. However, if you see others around who aren't having as good a day, think about sharing your good fortune. Camping out at one spot all day without letting others have a chance can be a little greedy. Consider sharing with others. It has a way of coming back to you one way or another.

Don't Leave Folks in Your Wake

IF YOU ARE fishing from a boat with a motor, be considerate of others on the water. As you begin to approach other anglers or boaters, throttle down the engine. If anglers are wading, a large wake can swamp their waders or cause them to lose their footing. It could also cause a kayaker to lose control.

Watch Where You Float

IF YOU ARE in a boat or kayak and approach a wading angler, consider the direction you will take when passing. The best thing to do is ask the angler if they prefer that you go in front or behind. In most cases they won't care, but just the fact that you have asked shows that you are being responsible and polite.

Watch for Redds

DURING TIMES WHEN fish are spawning, they create spawning beds known as redds, as discussed in Chapter 16. These are typically in shallow gravel areas. You can identify the redds by the scooped out areas that look like little indentations in the river bed. The redds are easy to spot since the gravel there will look a little brighter than that of the surrounding area. The beds are full of trout eggs, so it's important not to walk through the redd. Pay close attention to where you are walking so that you don't crush the eggs or small fry that may be holding in the gravel. This will ensure future fish for many more seasons.

Offer Up a Good Word

IF YOU HAVE had an exceptionally good day, why not share the joy? There are a lot of fish in the river. If you come across a fellow fly fisher who is struggling, consider letting them know what worked for you. I've known folks who are extremely tight-lipped about the flies they are using. Of course, we all have those secret weapons that we want to keep close to the vest, but it never hurts to share a little of the wealth.

Keep Quiet on the Numbers

FLY FISHING IS challenging, so when you dial in on the right fly and everything comes together for you, of course you want to shout it from the rooftops. However, the proper etiquette when sharing your good fortune with other anglers is to withhold the count. Let's say a drift boat comes by with a guide and two clients. The guide has worked tirelessly all day with these two beginners, and it's been a slow afternoon. The guide feels fortunate that they have boated two fish because the beginners have struggled with fly delivery and hook sets. The beginners are thrilled to have each caught their first trout. As they float by, they say hello and ask about your day. You in turn, proudly boast, "I've caught 45 fish. The fish are eating anything I cast to them. How about you?" Each member of the boat congratulates you, but they are left feeling deflated. The better response from you could have been something like, "Well, a bad day on the river is better than a good day at work. My zebra midges have fooled a few fish today. It's just fun being on the water."

Pick Up Your Trash

THIS SEEMS OBVIOUS, but I'm always amazed and disheartened by the amount of trash I see left along the river's edge. I commonly will see leftover worm containers and lure packaging. Occasionally I will find fishing line that has been pulled from a reel and just left on the bank. I can't help but wonder about the people who do this. Who do they think will come behind them and pick up this stuff? We can all do our part. Be sure to pack out whatever you bring in. I often keep an empty trash bag in the car and pick up items that I find along the river. It doesn't seem to put a dent in all the trash that's out there, but every little bit counts.

Catch and Release

I WOULD VENTURE TO say that the vast majority of fly fishers are catch-and-release anglers. The true reward isn't a trout dangling on a stringer but the satisfaction of discovering a productive body of water, presenting the right fly in just the right spot, and setting the hook at the precise moment to land and admire the beautiful fish. With the popularity of fishing and new anglers attracted to the sport each season, it's possible the resources could be depleted quickly. If everyone kept their limit of fish, there wouldn't be too many more catching days left in a season. Lee Wulff was one of the primary proponents of catch-and-release fishing. He was known to have said, "The finest gift you can give to any fisherman is to put a good fish back, and who knows if the fish you caught isn't someone else's gift to you."

CHAPTER 18

Bodies of Water

F YOU ARE lucky enough to have someone in your life who gives constant encouragement as you pursue your goals and dreams, then you will understand what Debra Skelly was for me. She was my administrative assistant at Parsons Brinckerhoff for many years and was one of the dearest people in my life. Sadly, she passed away recently, but during the course of our years working together, I would share stories with her about work and personal experiences. She used to tell me that I lead a charmed life and that she had never met anyone who lived constantly "in the zone." Thinking about it still makes me smile. I don't know about living a charmed life, but I am indeed blessed in so many ways. I count having her as a friend a major blessing.

So, as Debra would say, 2010 was definitely an "in the zone" year. Nikki and I had spent many fishing trips and dinners talking about how we both wanted to turn our dreams into reality. Of course, my dream was to build a fly fishing school on the river and eventually retire from engineering, turning my passion into a full-time endeavor.

Nikki's dream was to find an old building she could renovate, where she could open a café featuring live music. She was an excellent cook and wanted to share her recipes and love of music with Middle Tennessee. As I mentioned earlier, Nikki's life was magical. As a pilot, in 1998, Nikki and her dear friend Rhonda Miles flew a single-engine plane around the world. The trip traced the flight path of the historic *Rodina* ("motherland"), which three female Russian combat pilots flew from Moscow to Siberia before World War II. Nikki was quoted after the trip as saying, "Fear to me now is just the place I haven't been yet." (Visit bridgeof wings.com for more information on Nikki's flight around the world.)

Nikki somehow made the most outrageous dreams a reality. Not only did she have the amazing experience of the Russia flight, but she was also the business manager for Waylon Jennings. It seemed anything she could visualize in her mind would develop into action. I watched it happen many times. Coincidentally, our dreams started to materialize at the same time.

One day, I was kayaking down the Caney Fork River with my friend Top and looked over at the bank to see a large AUCTION sign in an empty field. I had always wanted to find property on the Caney Fork but had never seriously looked. When I got home, I called to find out more details about the auction. It sounded promising, so I went back to the river and walked the property, looking at the different lots that would be for sale. I decided the time was right, and I would attend the auction.

When I arrived, a large white tent was set up, and quite a few people were already there. I had a chance to talk with the auctioneer before the bidding began and asked a million questions. I was nervous because I had never purchased anything at an auction, and a 20%, non-refundable deposit was required, followed by closing within 30 days. I would have been happy to have purchased any of the lots that day, but I was fortunate enough to be the highest bidder on the exact lot I really wanted. The developer, Brock Rust, seemed just as excited for me to buy the land as I was to get it. As I was signing the papers at the close of the auction, I asked Brock if I could spend a little time fishing in

SOUTHERN BROOKIES FLY FISHING SCHOOL ON THE CANEY FORK RIVER

the river. Because it would be 30 days before the property was actually mine, I didn't know if he would let me. He was gracious enough to say yes, so I put on my waders and headed down to the water.

I'll never forget the magic of that day. I landed over 20 trout in a 2-hour period. It was as if they were welcoming their new neighbor. It literally seemed that I caught a fish on every cast. The day far exceeded my wildest dreams to be the owner of this beautiful piece of land.

During the same month, Nikki found her dream building in the little town of Normandy, Tennessee. It had been an old hardware store with a wonderful second-floor living space. Just as she had imagined, she could live on the second floor and use the spacious first floor for the café. It was the perfect spot for Nikki's dream. The building was fortuitously located near two trout-filled tailwaters: the Duck River, only 20 minutes away, and the Elk River, which could be reached in under 45 minutes. So here we were, watching our dreams beginning to take shape just minutes away from three of the best trout-filled tailwaters in the Middle Tennessee area.

I was telling this story to a great client and friend recently, and she asked if I could give her the definition of a tailwater. She had heard the term but wasn't sure if she really knew the difference in the various bodies of water. This started me thinking that many fly fishers are probably in the same boat. So thank you, Susan Doll, for being the inspiration for this next section!

Tailwater

A TAILWATER IS A body of water located immediately below a dammed reservoir or lake. Sometimes the dams are constructed to provide electricity; water from the lake is released through gates in the dam, causing the turbines to operate and generate power. Other times the dams are used for flood control, so the water release is

MUSIC CITY FLY GIRL TERI BAINBRIDGE FISHES ON THE ROARING FORK RIVER, A FAMOUS
FREESTONE IN COLORADO.

regulated based on the lake level. In either case, the river below the
dam is known as a tailwater. If the water release is through a spillway,
the temperature will typically be too high to support trout since the
ideal water temperature for trout is 45–65°F. However, if the water is
released from the base of the dam, it's a different story. The cold water
from the depths of the lake make it possible for trout to thrive. The
speed and depth of the water will be determined by the amount of
water being released from the dam.

Freestone

A FREESTONE BODY OF water is formed as snow begins to melt and
form small streams. The water flows along a streambed of gravel
and boulders. The streams will have a relatively steep gradient with
plunging pools and fast-moving runs. Snow runoff and rain are the
main water sources so, as you can imagine, the flow levels will vary

THE MUSIC CITY FLY GIRLS FISHING THE SAN JUAN RIVER, A WELL-KNOWN TAILWATER
Photographed by Deb Paschall

based on the weather. During times of drought, the stream levels will be very low, and during wet years the streams are filled to capacity. Because the streams begin in the upper elevations with the melting snow, the water temperature is ideal for trout. As the stream increases in size and begins to flow to lower elevations, the water temperature may rise to a level that will not support trout. Typically, the best time for trout fishing a freestone stream is late spring to early summer and also in the fall. This is when you will find the water temperatures and current flows to be ideal for hungry trout.

A good example illustrating both a freestone stream and a tailwater is the beautiful San Juan River. The headwaters of the San Juan begin in the high elevations of the Rocky Mountains in southwestern Colorado where two freestones come together: the East Fork and the West Fork. The combined waters then flow through the foothills into the Navajo Reservoir, which is impounded by Navajo Dam, and the tailwaters of the San Juan River flow just below the dam.

The Music City Fly Girls fished the San Juan River during the summer of 2018. We flew into Albuquerque and rented a large van for

GUIDING ANDY MICHAEL ON ONE OF MY ALL-TIME FAVORITE SPRINGS CREEKS—A TOP SECRET SPOT

the 3-hour drive to Fisheads San Juan River Lodge in Navajo Dam, New Mexico. I've fished many rivers over the course of my fly fishing career, and I believe this river is one of the prettiest. The water is crystal clear, which allows you to see enormous trout just waiting to take your fly. I can't wait to go back. I highly recommend Fisheads lodge if you decide to visit. The guides are top-notch, the food is excellent, and it's hard to beat the convenience.

Spring Creek

THE SOURCE OF water for a spring creek comes from an underground aquifer. This is where water seeps into porous rocks. Think of the rock like a large sponge soaking up water. This contained water is known as groundwater. When this groundwater reaches the surface, it's known as a spring. The water temperature from emerging springs can be hot or very cold. As fly fishers, we are most interested in springs with cold water, which support trout. These creeks can be tough to fish since they are clear as glass and often have overhanging

HOT CREEK IN THE HIGH SIERRAS

limbs that can make casting challenging. The water movement typically results from the pressure from the water coming to the surface, as opposed to gravity pulling water down a steep grade as seen with freestone streams. This results in a more gently moving current. Without the turbulent flow to help conceal our presence, extra stealth is required. This is what makes it a great challenge, and it's my personal favorite type of water to fish.

One of my all-time favorite Music City Fly Girls trips was to the High Sierras. I talk about this trip a bit more in Chapter 28, "Packing for a Fly Fishing Trip," but it's worth mentioning here since it fits in nicely with the spring creek discussion. One of the areas where we fished was Hot Creek. This is one of those places with scenery that will literally take your breath away. The makeup of Hot Creek is fascinating. The uppermost section is formed by three springs that have a consistent temperature of 60°F. The Hot Creek Hatchery is located in this area and uses the water from the three springs for its facility, as the consistent temperature is ideal for fish production. As the water leaves

GEOTHERMAL AREA OF HOT CREEK

the facility, it becomes Hot Creek. Just a short distance below the hatchery, Hot Creek merges with the freestone known as Mammoth Creek. As the spring creek (Hot Creek) and the freestone (Mammoth Creek) merge, they maintain the name Hot Creek. The private and public areas downstream of the merging waters offer some excellent trout fishing.

Approximately 5 miles downstream of the hatchery is a beautiful, turquoise geothermal area where the water temperature reaches levels far too high for trout. At one time, people were allowed to swim in this heated section. However, due to unexpected spikes in temperatures, swimming is no longer allowed. Still, it remains an amazing location to visit and to fish. Don't be surprised if you spend as much time taking pictures and taking in the scenery as you do wetting a line.

Knowing the various classifications of water bodies is an important part of your fly fishing education. This information will help you to select the most appropriate gear and flies, and to determine the best techniques to use.

CHAPTER 19

Reading the Waters

Looking back to the late fall of 2010, Southern Brookies and The River Café were doing amazingly well. My casting classes and guide calendar were both full. Nikki's café was "the place to be in Normandy." She was being written up in numerous articles touting the food and live entertainment. With her signature whiskey bread pudding and her brother Mike's mouthwatering brisket, folks were more than happy to make the 90-minute drive from Nashville to enjoy the experience.

In addition, the Music City Fly Girls were celebrating four strong years since the formation of the club. We had more than 40 members on the roster, most of whom were very active in the monthly meetings and scheduled outings. Our volunteer work with Casting for Recovery (see page 269) was featured on *Tennessee's Wild Side,* an Emmy-winning television program. The local fly fishing shops were encouraging many of their female customers to look into what we had to offer. We were thankful and proud of all that was beginning to bloom and grow for us.

Then, like a hidden boulder under dark waters, the news that literally buckled my knees and caused me to reach more deeply into my faith than ever before hit us all during December 2010. Nikki had been diagnosed with pancreatic cancer.

Nikki had faced some scary and difficult challenges before, but this? This was indeed new and unwelcome territory. She bravely faced the challenges of that terrible disease that lay ahead of her. For the Music City Fly Girls, it seemed so surreal that this was all happening to our precious friend. We were all hurting and full of questions. How could this happen to someone so special, someone so caring, and someone just realizing the start of her lifelong dream? However, in true Nikki style, she was able to comfort and inspire all of us, determined that 6 months, as given by the doctor, was far too short a time to finish her story.

It's fascinating to me how our lives can be compared to a river, the twists and turns, the ebbs and flows, each with a beginning and an end. Unlike life, however, the river gives us clues as to what lies beneath the surface or what may be in store for us around the bend. You just need to know how and where to look.

Reading the Waters

To be successful on the water, you need to know where the fish are holding. This starts with an understanding of a trout's basic needs: safety against predators; comfort related to the speed of the current, oxygen, and temperature; and an ample supply of food. With this understanding, the next step is to dissect the river and identify the holding spots that provide these essentials. Understanding the water will go a long way in improving your hookup rate.

The river can be broken into four sections: riffles, runs, pools, and flats. Let's unpack each section.

Riffles

This segment of the river is characterized by its fast-moving, choppy water and is typically 1–3 feet deep. Riffles are a prime location for trout, as they provide the essential needs of food and safety. The shallow depth allows more sunlight to penetrate the water and promotes vegetation growth. This in turn supports a healthy aquatic insect population. The choppy surface of the water protects trout by providing a sort of camouflage, making it difficult for predators to see down through the water. This is also a plus for the fly fisher in that trout can't see up through the water because their cone of vision is limited when they are closer to the surface. The rocky bottom also provides some limited protection from the fast-moving currents. In these

THE MUSIC CITY FLY GIRLS ON THE BANKS OF THE MADISON RIVER, WITH A BEAUTIFUL, READY-TO-FISH RIFFLE FLOWING IN THE BACKGROUND

areas, the trout will move quickly to take food, so the fly imitation doesn't need to be an exact match of the actual insect.

On riffles, keep an eye out for pocket water, or the cushion of water behind or in front of a rock or structure that breaks the current. Fish will hold in these areas for protection against the current and lie in wait for food to drift by.

Run

A RUN IS DEEPER than a riffle (typically 3–6 feet deep), with a much slower current and a relatively smooth water surface. The deeper water provides safety against predators, and the slower current means the trout will expend less energy. With the slower current, the trout also has more time to inspect the fly. Thus, a closer imitation of the natural insect is needed. Anglers should pay special attention to slow and fast currents coming together. The lines where these currents meet are known as seams. The seams tend to collect insects and serve

NONIE SANDERS, ANGELA MILLET, AND DEB PASCHALL GETTING READY TO FISH THIS
ENTICING RUN ON THE MADISON RIVER

as a conveyor belt or buffet line for the trout. There are times when the
seams can also be recognized by a bubble or foam line. Insects congregate in these lines, so the area should be fished fully. Rocks and boulders, which break the current, will also typically be found throughout
runs. These are prime holding areas. And don't forget to watch for
structures such as a root ball, undercuts in the bank, or fallen limbs.
The three needs—safety, comfort, and food—are met in these areas, so
fish are certain to select these prime spots.

Pools

POOLS ARE DEEPER than runs, and the current is much slower. At
times, it may seem to be standing still. The trout will find protection in the depths of the pool, and less energy is needed to hold in
the slow, lazy currents. Food comes to the trout in even larger serving
sizes. Pools may hold sculpins, leeches, and crayfish, which explains
why large fish hold in these areas. There is plenty of time for the fish to

FISHING A BEAUTIFUL POOL NEAR CHARLOTTESVILLE, VIRGINIA

study the fly, so realistic presentations are key. Pools can be further sub-divided into three sections: the head of the pool is where a run or riffle feeds into it, the body is the deepest and slowest section, and the tailout is where the pool begins to climb from the depths and breaks out into the riffle or run just below the pool. If you begin fishing the body of the pool first, you may spook fish holding at the head or tailouts. Take your time and work the pool thoroughly upstream, from the tail to the head.

Flats

FLATS CAN BE successful areas to fish when bugs are hatching, but they can also be very challenging. These areas are clear and shallow with little cover for protection. Flats are similar to riffles in depth (1–4 feet), but they have a smooth and even bottom. The current can vary from slow to fast and, with limited cover, the fish will spook eas-ily. A precise presentation is key when fishing these areas.

Fish are opportunistic and will move in and out of these areas based on their needs, the time of day, and the seasons. Taking the time to study these areas and knowing how to fish them will give you more chance at success than just casting and hoping. Keep in mind the three basic needs of safety, comfort, and food. If you find areas that have a concentration of all these elements, your chances of finding the primary holding and feeding areas of the trout are very good.

So, before charging into the water the next time you are out fishing, take a minute and study the surface. Look for the seams and pocket water. Try to find those large, hidden boulders under the surface. There are hidden gems holding in those quiet spaces, and it's up to you to look closely and mine them out.

A PRECISE PRESENTATION IS KEY WHEN FISHING FLATS BECAUSE THE FISH SPOOK EASILY IN THE CLEAR, SHALLOW WATERS THAT OFFER THEM LITTLE PROTECTION.

CHAPTER 20

Setting the Hook

Nikki was a true warrior in every sense of the word as she battled her illness. She loved life, and she didn't let the fact that it was being cut short stop her from enjoying every second of the time she had remaining with her friends and family. Although she had been through a painful surgery, followed by weeks of chemotherapy that seemed to cripple her body, her spirit never wavered. During one of my visits with her, she asked what trip I was planning for the upcoming season. I told her we were going to White Fish, Montana. Her eyes lit up, and she boldly stated, "Well, that's my carrot for battling through this thing. Count me in on that one." Her body was so frail, and the trip was six months away. I secretly wondered how in the world she would feel well enough to make it but, in true Nikki fashion, she did it and made the trip even more special for us all.

We boarded a flight from Nashville to Seattle and made our way to The Arctic Club Seattle, a DoubleTree hotel, located near Pike Place Market. We were impressed by the beautiful hotel, which was formerly a social club for Arctic explorers. The next morning we had time for breakfast and to shop around a little. I had a chance to take everyone to

THE MUSIC CITY FLY GIRLS AT THE ARCTIC CLUB HOTEL

NIKKI ENJOYING HER ROOMETTE ON THE TRAIN

my favorite little Seattle shop, a bookstore called Peter Miller. It's definitely worth a visit if you are ever in the area.

Time passed quickly, and before we knew it, it was time to board the train. I had booked roomettes for us on Amtrak's *Empire Builder* for the overnight trip to Montana. We were so excited as we dropped our bags off and headed for dinner in the diner. It was truly a magical evening.

The next morning, we arrived in Whitefish, Montana, refreshed and ready to go. As our train pulled into the station, we were wide-eyed, looking at the little Western town surrounded by mountain peaks in the distance. We made our way to Lakestream Fly Shop to finalize plans for our float trip the next day. Seven boatloads of Music City Fly Girls filled the Flat Head River that next morning. It was a beautiful, sunny day, and we all had a blast. The day was spent nymphing, a technique we were accustomed to from our time on our own Middle Tennessee tailwaters. I shared a boat with Nikki that day and enjoyed seeing the bend in her rod as she stood up front in the casting braces. I remember feeling such admiration and inspiration for the way she was facing the greatest battle of her life with such gusto and grace.

The next day, part of the group decided to take a tour of Glacier National Park instead of fishing, so I was on my own for the day's float trip. I didn't mind at all, especially since the day turned out to be perfect for dry fly fishing late in the afternoon. I had certainly spent time with a dry fly in my fishing career, but the majority of my fishing

NIKKI PLAYS A FEISTY TROUT ON THE FLAT HEAD RIVER.

had been indicator fishing with nymphs or with streamers. My guide fixed me up with a small parachute Adams, and I proceeded to miss fish after fish. He would give out a little *bloop* with each rising fish, meaning I had just missed another. How could this be? I was too slow on setting the hook? I had always heard that you say, in your mind, "God save the queen" to give plenty of time for the fish to take the fly. Well, obviously this wasn't the case with these Flat Head trout. They were quick that day, and I was slow. I remember managing to land a couple, but I missed many, many more.

The group reconvened that evening for a late Mexican dinner before heading off to catch the midnight train to Portland, Oregon. We were sad to leave Whitefish behind, but the next morning, as we caught our first glimpse of Portland from the train windows, a new wave of emotion overtook us. A new city with a full day ahead to explore! We checked into our little boutique hotel, Kimpton Hotel Monaco, before making our way out to dinner. To our amazement,

A Quick-Reference Color Guide to **Common Flies** and **Fish**

Flies by Kam Koleas

Adams

This traditional dry fly has been around a long time and is a true classic. It's a great searching fly, as it imitates a wide range of insects. The original design has been modified a number of times, so don't be surprised to see a wide variety available. It's one of the most popular and effective dry flies, so pick up a handful in sizes 10-20.

Griffith's Gnat

This impressionistic fly can imitate an adult midge when fished in smaller sizes and resembles a cluster of midges when tied on larger hooks. I often use a larger Griffith's gnat with a Thrasher's Magic Midge for a dry fly dropper setup.

Bead-Head Pheasant Tail

This is one of my favorite patterns. It's an impressionistic pattern that can imitate stone fly or mayfly nymphs. They are typically tied on a 2X long nymph hook, but I've had great success tying larger pheasant tails on scud hooks and using a bit of flash for the wing case.

Frenchie

This pattern is basically a fancy pheasant tail with a hot spot tied in at the collar. I'm a big fan of this fly tied on a jig hook with a pink collar in size 14.

Mopfly

I have used this fly on both cold- and warm-water rivers and lakes and have caught trout, bream, carp, catfish, crappie, and bass. Tied on larger hooks like a size 4, they tend to resemble a threadfin shad. Smaller sizes can imitate scuds and crane fly larva. When tied in green, they look similar to the green inchworm or caddis larva.

Neversink Caddis

With its yellow foam body, this dry fly is extremely buoyant and easy to follow as it moves through the plunge pools of the mountain streams. This attractor will imitate both caddis flies and yellow stone flies.

Gardner's Never Bug

This is a very buggy fly and one of my favorites. I think of it like an everything bagel for a trout. It looks like the best parts of a hare's ear and pheasant tail combined. It's very messy, very heavy, and very effective.

Thrasher's Magic Midge

With just four components (a size 14 scud hook, black thread, a silver tungsten bead, and a little Thrasher magic), this is one of the simplest flies imaginable. The slender profile is the key characteristic. I consider it an impressionistic pattern, as it can replicate a small leech, black fly larva, midge larva, or snail.

Woolly Bugger

This fly is considered a streamer. Streamer flies are tied to resemble baitfish; leeches; minnows; crayfish; and other long, slender food sources. The Woolly Bugger is also a favorite winter fly.

Eat at Chuck's

This is a soft-hackle fly designed by my friend Chuck Robinson. I've used this fly throughout Tennessee and on many trips out West with great success. It's intended to be fished in the surface film and can be dead-drifted or stripped at varying speeds. My favorites are in sizes 14 and 16.

Pat's Rubber Legs

I consider this an imitative fly. I believe it has a striking resemblance to the natural insect, and it's one of my favorites. I find it most effective when tied with a tungsten bead, which helps it reach depth quickly in fast-moving currents.

Zebra Midge

This simple imitative pattern has worked in almost every river I have fished. It typically is tied in sizes 14 and smaller. I fish it below a strike indicator, often in tandem with another zebra midge or similar midge. They can be fished deep in the water column, imitating a larva, or in the surface film, imitating a midge pupa.

Brook Trout

This is a beautifully colored fish with wormy markings along the back, and dark-olive sides scattered with red spots encircled by blue halos. The leading edge of the pectoral, pelvic, and anal fins is tipped in white. The tail fin is less forked than that of other trout; thus, the fish is sometimes called a squaretail.

Brown Trout

This trout is typically golden brown with large brown or black spots, and occasional red spots, on its sides. The belly is a lighter yellow. The spots are often surrounded by light-colored halos. The tail typically does not have spots; if any exist, they are very light and are only on the top half.

Rainbow Trout

The coloring of a rainbow trout is a unique combination of greens, blues, and yellows. These fish are darker along the upper part of the body, with the color softening along the sides and becoming off-white or silver along the belly. They are covered with dark spots from head to tail. The rainbow trout's most distinctive feature is the pinkish-red band along its side. The pink band becomes more brilliant around the time of spawning.

THE MUSIC CITY FLY GIRLS ABOUT TO BOARD THE TRAIN TO PORTLAND

the rooms were full of paintings with fly fishers, and not just any fly fishers, but women! What a treat!

The next morning, we saved time for a quick trip to Voodoo Doughnut and Stumptown Coffee, some of the best coffee in the world, before heading back to Nashville. That trip will forever be in my memory. Nikki grabbed her proverbial carrot, friendship bonds were deepened, and the trip was an overall success. All of these were wonderful memories, except for the small nagging memory of all the fish I missed with those improper hook sets. I am due a trip back to redeem myself.

VOODOO DOUGHNUT IS A REQUIRED STOP WHEN THE FLY GIRLS VISIT PORTLAND.

Hook Sets

IT ONLY TAKES a split second for the fish to feel and taste the metal of a hook and realize it isn't the meaty morsel that was imagined. Once this deception is detected, the hook is spit out with lightning speed. Our challenge is to gauge the timing between when the trout sets its eye on the food, attacks the potential meal, and then detects that it is a fraud. Setting the hook was covered briefly in Chapter 15 (page 138), but it's worth taking a deeper dive into the action based on the fishing technique you are using.

INDICATOR FISHING

INDICATORS ARE EXACTLY as described. They give you an indication as to when a fish is interested in your offering. As the indicator floats along naturally with the current, even the smallest bump or swirl of the current will affect its movement. It's critical to watch the indicator intently, and if it slows down, stops, makes a jerky movement, or goes under, the hook must be set immediately. Any hesitation, and the fish will most likely be gone. Lifting the rod tip straight up or downstream will most often hook the fish in the top or side edge of the lip. Keep in mind that the fish are facing upstream, waiting on food to come their way. If you set the hook with an upstream motion, you are snatching the fly right from their mouths. So, be very aware of the hook set direction. The hook set is an action requiring a keen eye and quick reflexes. For some odd reason, if you happen to look around for a moment at the scenery or lift your hand to scratch your nose, that is the exact moment the indicator will disappear. Ask any fly fisher about this, and they will tell you it's true. It's like the fish know you have been distracted, and that's the exact time they will strike, so pay attention. This reminds me of fishing with my favorite fly fishing buddy of all time, my sister, Cindy. One day on the Caney Fork River, she was reaching for a bottle of water and missed a fish. Then she was reaching to eat a Funyun and missed another fish. Each miss was when she looked away for a split

CINDY WITH A NICE BROWN AFTER A FEW "FUNYUN" MISSES

second. We still laugh about this and, to this day, if I see someone miss a fish because of being distracted, I call it a Funyun.

Dry Fly

A DRY FLY hook set isn't the same for every situation. I have fished top-water flies where you literally had to wait three seconds before setting the hook. That's where saying "God save the queen" in your mind helps you slow down and wait for the take to actually occur. Then there are other times when you have to be lightning fast with your reflexes to make it work. I remember one time fishing with my good friend and neighbor John Parrish. I had just cast a large hopper to the side of the bank when I saw a wake moving toward the fly. Then I saw the jaws open wide and inhale the fly. It was all I could do to watch it all unfold before lifting the rod tip and setting the hook on what would be an enormous, monster brown trout. The key is knowing your fish and how they are feeding, and then adjusting the hook set timing to match.

THE BROWN THAT WAS WORTH THE WAIT

STREAMER

STREAMER FISHING IS a different story altogether when setting the hook. You will want to keep your rod tip down when drifting, swinging, or stripping in the fly. Once the fish takes the fly, the tendency will be to move the rod to a straight-up position. Fight the urge to do this. If you miss, you will pull the fly too far away from the fish for a second chance. If you continue stripping and make what is called a strip set, you have a much better chance of properly hooking the fish in the jaw as it attacks the swimming prey. Likewise, if the trout misses the fly, the fly is still in the fish's feeding zone, and there is a chance it will come back for a second bite. I've had numerous experiences where it takes not just one or two swipes but several before the fish actually commits and eats the fly.

Streamer fishing is hard to beat. It's aggressive, and there is no mistaking the hit. I have my good friend and fellow guide David Perry with Southeastern Fly to thank for showing me this proper technique. It took a while to get out of the habit of raising my rod tip, but I finally caught on. I remember distinctly, one day while we were fishing together, feeling a fish bump the fly and setting the hook with a very long and deliberate strip set. I heard David say, "Now that's how you set the hook." He didn't know it then, but that comment made the day for me.

When streamer fishing, be sure to keep your rod as low as possible. I actually keep my rod tip a few inches below the surface of the water. I know this may sound odd, but it works. Having the tip in the water helps keep you perfectly connected with the fly, meaning slack line is eliminated.

Different techniques and fishing situations require frequent changes. Test it out. Work on your timing and learn from the misses because trial and error is the absolute best instructor.

CHAPTER 21

A Few of My Favorite Things

Fortunately for me, the Music City Fly Girls all seem to enjoy shopping for gear as much as I do. During our annual trips and outings, we have our traditional stops along the way. We don't travel through Maryville, Tennessee, without stopping by Little River Trading Company, especially during their winter sale in the spring. Then, of course, there is the stop by Little River Outfitters in Townsend to see Daniel, Byron, and sometimes Paula, if she isn't focusing on her chef skills. This is one of the best fly shops around, and they always have great tips for fishing in the Smokies.

But one of our all-time favorite stops is at Dally's Ozark Fly Fisher in Cotter, Arkansas, as we make our way to the White River each October. They have a huge inventory of gear, and we can't wait to get inside.

One year, I was looking through the glass case at Dally's, which holds some of the items they have on consignment. My eyes landed on a beautiful Swiss fly-tying vise by Marc Petitjean. It looked more like a piece of art than a fly-tying tool, and I was fascinated by the design.

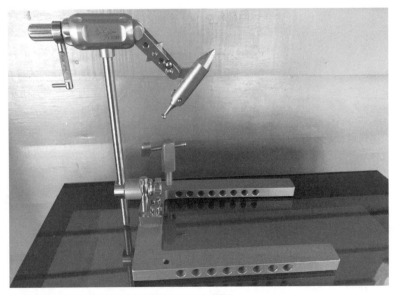

A THOUGHTFUL GIFT FROM THE MUSIC CITY FLY GIRLS

I walked away three or four times, returning several times to study the intricate details. I had no idea anyone was watching me, but Fly Girl Susan Henderson noticed. She mentioned it to the other Fly Girls later on during the trip. Without my knowing about it, they slipped back to the shop and bought that vise. Just a few months later, at the Music City Fly Girls Christmas party, the club gave me the vise as a gift. It was such a special moment, and I was completely surprised by their kindness. It truly demonstrated the thoughtful and giving nature of our club members. I treasure that vise and use it on a weekly basis.

This vise is one of my many favorite fly fishing items. When I find a great piece of gear or clothing, I usually spread the word. In fact, if you study any of the pictures of the Music City Fly Girls in any great detail, you may see us in the same gear and clothing.

Here are a few favorites that you might want to add to your own wish list. You may recognize a couple of items from Chapter 2, but I believe they bear repeating.

HARDY BROOK BAG (SIMILAR TO THE HBX ALN BAG) AND TILLEY WINTER HAT (SIMILAR TO THE TTW2 TEC-WOOL HAT)

- **HARDY HBX ALN BAG** This is a handsome little over-the-shoulder bag that is very versatile. It can be used as a book bag or out on the river to hold fly boxes, leader, and tippet. It has a classic look and gets better-looking the more you use it. *hardyfishing.com*

- **TILLEY TTW2 TEC-WOOL HAT** This is a great-looking hat to wear on the river or just around town on a blustery day. On extra-cold and windy days, you can pull down the ear flaps that are tucked inside the hat. It comes in a variety of colors, but I like the Rust. *tilley.com*

- **ABEL NIPPERS** Nippers are one of the most frequently used items in a gear bag. Cheap ones wear out quickly. The Abel nippers are guaranteed for two years and, if they happen to go dull during that time, the company will replace the jaws at no charge. They are a little pricey, but they really work and have lasted longer than any others I've tried. If you

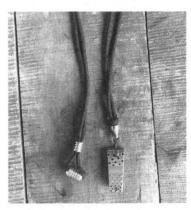

ABEL NIPPERS

are feeling extra generous or deserving, check out the nippers with the trout graphics. They are truly a work of art. *abelreels.com*

- **DYNAMICS OF FLY CASTING VIDEO BY JOAN WULFF** Joan Wulff is arguably one of the best fly fishing instructors of all time. In this video, she demonstrates the casting techniques she has been developing and refining for many years. This is a must have for any fly fishing video library. I can't begin to count the times I've watched it. *royalwulff.com/products/dynamics-of-fly-casting-dvd*

- **PATAGONIA NANO PUFF JACKET** (patagonia.com) This is a wind- and water-resistant jacket that comes in both pullover and full-zip styles. It is a great piece to layer with or to use on its own. When you put it on, it feels like sliding into a down sleeping bag. One of the

HARDY ULTRALITE REEL

best things about this jacket is that it packs down to almost nothing, allowing you to slip it into your fishing vest until you need some extra warmth. The jacket comes in a variety of colors. *patagonia.com*

● **HARDY ULTRALITE FLY REELS** I first noticed this reel on my friend Alice Russell's rod and did a double take. It was one of the best-looking reels I had ever seen. It is beautifully designed, light-weight, and, being a Hardy, obviously well crafted. This is a great reel from a renowned manufacturer at a remarkable value. *hardyfishing.com*

● **FILSON FOUL WEATHER FLY FISHING VEST** This vest is a true workhorse and gets better-looking with age. There are numerous pockets designed to hold all your gear. I especially like the large zip pocket in the back for carrying a small thermos of coffee, a sack lunch, and my Nano Puff jacket. The Filson brand is hard to beat. *filson.com*

● **CHOTA HIPPIES** Sometimes you don't need to wear your full wad-ers, especially when fishing from the kayak or in a shallow creek. On days when it's too cold to wet wade and you need to keep your feet dry, these convertible waders are the perfect solution. They adjust to three lengths: knee high, just above the knee, and hip level. *chotaoutdoorgear.com*

FILSON FOUL WEATHER FLY FISHING VEST

● **A. D. MADDOX FLY BOX** (See page 22 for photo.) A. D. Maddox is a native of Nashville, Tennessee, and a brilliant artist. She recently moved to Livingston, Montana, where she has opened her own studio. The Montana Fly Company has used a number of her trout-skin prints on their fly boxes. The brook trout is my favorite—so much so, that I purchased the art from her to wrap my little vintage camper. Thanks, A. D.! *montanafly.com*

● **C&F DESIGN MARCO POLO FLY-TYING SYSTEM** This is one of the best sets of tools I own. The set is compact enough to slip easily into my bag for out-of-town trips and comes in a self-contained box, securely holding a vise, a bobbin with three thread colors, scissors, a whip-finish tool, and a few other tools to round out the kit. It's a little pricey, but it's high quality, and you'll have it for a lifetime. *us.seriousfishing .com/CFDESIGN0307573.html*

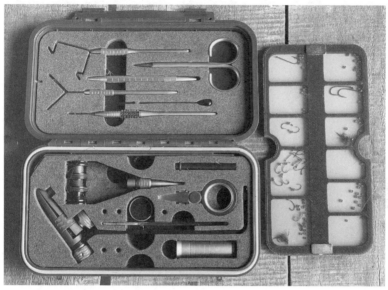

C&F DESIGN MARCO POLO FLY-TYING SYSTEM

• **FISHPOND NOMAD NET** I absolutely love this net. It serves many purposes for me besides its intended one of safely netting the fish. I have used it as a wading staff, to free hooks from obstructions, and to clear paths through brush and briars. I purchased the optional end cap that fits over the handle. This adds a little protection to the handle and gives extra traction when using it as a wading staff. *fishpondusa.com*

FISHPOND NOMAD NET

• **SIMMS TACO BAG** The Taco is a great way to keep your gear together. I keep my waders and boots in

THE SIMMS TACO IS GREAT FOR STORING WET BOOTS AND WADERS AFTER A DAY OF FISHING.

this slender bag. Once I reach my destination, it fully unzips to give me a dry place to stand as I get into my waders. It's large enough to carry a rod, reel, and small pack. On several of the Music City Fly Girls trips, this has served as our carry-on bag. It fits perfectly in the overhead bin. *simmsfishing.com*

● **PATAGONIA SPRING RIVER WOMEN'S WADERS** Honestly, I think half of our club owns these waders. They are, by far, the most comfortable waders I have ever owned. In fact, after a day of guiding, I once found myself upstairs at the cabin fixing dinner and realized I hadn't changed out of my gear. True story. They are made to fit women and, as a bonus, they are figure-flattering. It may seem odd to say that about fishing waders, but somehow Patagonia manages it with this design. *patagonia.com*

These are some of my very favorite fly fishing treasures. Your local fly shop will carry many of these items, so show your hometown support while shopping.

CHAPTER 22

Tips on Improving Your Hookups

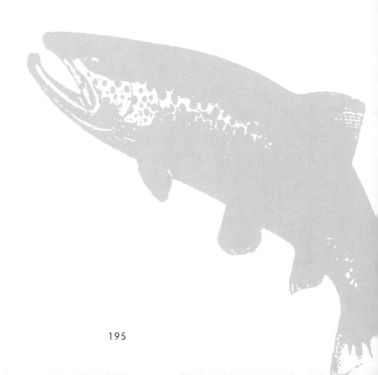

Have you ever been in the river, looking around at all the others who are catching fish while you haven't had a bump all day? Or you read the online posts after your own weekend "goose egg," and all the reports from others read, "We slammed them all day!" All the while you might have been thinking, "What was I doing wrong?"

During one of our Music City Fly Girls outings on the Caney Fork, there were a number of Fly Girls in this situation. We had been fishing throughout the weekend, and while a number of club members had caught their fair share, not everyone had been as fortunate. One of the best things about being a guide is being able to share the wisdom of countless days on the water. When you basically spend every waking moment fishing, you pick up some tricks that can really help with the catching part. I love being able to provide others with a few tips that can often help them turn their day around. On this particular weekend afternoon, I offered to take a few of the Fly Girls out individually in my tandem kayak. I spent about an hour with each one, and the smiles during that day made it all worthwhile.

I think we've all been there at one time or another. It's disheartening and very discouraging. But take heart! Sometimes it takes just a few slight adjustments to turn things around and lift your spirits.

The Perfect Drift

A well-presented fly will land on the water and swim or float just like a natural insect. If you cast your line into the water and

NANCY WITH A BEAUTIFUL CANEY FORK RIVER RAINBOW TROUT

the current takes over, the flies will drag behind like a water-skier being pulled by a boat, and your chances of fooling a fish will be greatly diminished. There are a couple of things you can do that will result in a drag-free drift.

• **WATER MEND** Typically, if you are fishing under an indicator, you will want the indicator to go downriver first, which means keeping your fly line upstream. After you cast and the line is on the water, lift your rod tip in a sweeping, semicircular motion, and gently toss the fly line upstream above the indicator. Don't worry if the indicator moves a little. The idea is to reposition the flies downstream, so mend like you really mean it. Remember, if the flies lag behind, the current takes over, and they will be pulled in an unnatural motion.

• **AERIAL MEND** This option is most easily accomplished with a reach cast: After making a stop on the forward cast, simply reach the rod upstream. The idea is to reposition the fly line upstream before it hits the water. You must slip line on the reach, so as not to shorten the presentation. The action of the fly is one of the most important steps in fly fishing. If you can get this right, you will see positive results.

Working on the drift was our area of focus the day that Nancy Wilcenski climbed into the kayak. It had been a while since she had been out on the river with us, so she was eager to get a few fish to the net. Since she was a little rusty, her presentation was causing the indicator and flies to drag along the surface. However, with just a few quick pointers, she positioned the fly line behind the indicator, which allowed the current to carry the fly like a natural insect. That's all it took that day for the catch rate to begin to improve.

Depth Matters

ALTHOUGH FISHING TOP water with dry flies is exciting, it isn't always the most productive technique. Studies show that fish feed subsurface 90% of the time, so if you are fishing with a dry fly, consider changing to a subsurface fly. The next step is determining the depth where the fish are feeding. Keep in mind that fish tend to gravitate toward the bottom of the river where the current is slow and they don't need to expend

JON JORDAN AND DAUGHTER ADDISON

much energy. Don't shy away from long leaders at depths that bounce flies along the bottom. We all get lazy, and yes, it takes time to adjust the indicator over and over, but if you have the patience to make the adjustments, the extra effort will result in more frequent hookups.

I was fishing with my good friend and excellent fly fisher Jon Jordan several years ago. We were on the Elk River in a deep section he rarely fished. I slowed down the drift boat, took the rod, and added a significant amount of tippet to the leader. At one point, we were fishing between 15 and 20 feet deep. Jon looked at me like I was crazy, but that look disappeared when we started catching fish as quickly as we could cast to them. Jon has brought up that lesson on long leaders many times since then, and we both know getting deep works wonders when the fish are hugging the bottom.

Put On a Little Weight

S OMETIMES THE WEIGHT of the fly isn't enough to get it down deep enough to reach where the fish are holding. Even if it's tied with a heavy bead head or a little lead in the body, sometimes it needs more help. To solve this problem, your best bet is to add a little split shot

SPLIT SHOT AND
TWIST LEAD

or twist lead to the leader. Personally, I'm not a fan of split shot. It's not too hard to attach them to the leader, but I always have trouble removing them. I opt for twist lead instead. This is a flat, thin strip of supple lead that easily twists around the leader. It's just as easy to get off as it is to put it on. If you attach the lead just above the knot connecting the final piece of tippet, then it won't slide down to the fly. I can't begin to count the times that adding a little weight to my setup immediately produced fish.

Change the Menu

WE ALL HAVE our favorite go-to flies. We have confidence that these flies will catch fish because they have worked before. However, there are times when the fish just aren't interested in what's being served, and you need to change it up. This doesn't mean going crazy and using every fly in your box. Stick with some of your trusted, tried-and-true patterns, but change it up a bit by trying a different size or color. I have used tiny zebra midges for years, but one season the tiny little guys weren't working for me. I jumped up several sizes larger, going from a size 20 to a 14, and wham! What a surprise. Sometimes, I believe that if a fish is going to go to the trouble of moving to eat a

CRAIG KNOWLES IS NOW A BELIEVER IN THE "PORK CHOP" FLY.

fly that's the size of a pin head, why not make it worth his while and give him a nice, meaty morsel instead.

Two of my favorite fly fishing friends, Craig and Sherry Knowles, were visiting with me one day on their way to a local fly fishing competition. If I remember correctly, it was a fundraiser and a beautiful Jackson kayak was the big prize for the angler catching the largest fish. In passing, I suggested giving my gigantic "pork chop" fly a try. Craig probably thought it was too big, so he tucked it away and decided not to use it. When they stopped back by later that afternoon, the competition had just wrapped up, and they told me that a 12-inch trout had won the prize for the largest fish. They decided to fish for a little longer that afternoon, and I urged Craig to give the behemoth fly a few tries. A little while later I heard a large cheer from the river and looked up in time to see Craig's rod with a huge bend in it. I was able to make it upstream in time to snap this shot. This would have taken the competition easily that day. Sometimes it pays to select "Yo Mamma's Platter" from the menu.

Move It

I F YOU GO to your favorite spot, and the fish aren't cooperating, you may have to wade farther up- or downstream to find the fish. Another angler may have been in your spot prior to your arrival, or a blue heron

may have been feeding in the area. Either situation could leave the fish tight-lipped. Covering a wide area throughout the day is often the ticket to finding the fish. During the Fly Girls' kayak fishing outing on the Caney Fork River, Lisa King had been fishing in one spot for most of the afternoon because the others were lined up and down the river. When it was her

LISA KING MOVED DOWNSTREAM TO FIND HER JEWEL.

turn for a few guide tips, I asked her to join me in the tandem kayak, and we were able to move a good ways downstream to an area that hadn't been fished that day. It only took a few casts to find the reward.

Get a Little Clearer

W HEN SELECTING LEADER and tippet material, monofilament is the most economical choice. However, investing a bit more in fluorocarbon will give you the added stealth that may often be necessary for wary trout. Fluorocarbon is extremely clear and almost invisible to fish. You may want to spend a few extra dollars to gain this advantage. I had clients on the water one weekend who were visiting

CINDY FOUND SUCCESS AFTER A LITTLE CASTING ADJUSTMENT.

from England. The angler in the front braces of my drift boat had a monofilament leader already rigged and was wanting to go ahead and use his own gear to get started. I obliged and left things the way they were and only tied on an indicator and fly. The other angler in the back of the boat had me start fresh with a new leader. I used a fluorocarbon leader and tippet. The angler in the back was outfishing his mate 10 to 1. When the angler in the front finally relinquished and changed to fluorocarbon, he quickly caught up to his friend. Both of them were fishing the same fly, depth, and indicator; however, the clarity of the leader and tippet made all the difference that day.

Check Your Flies

HOW OFTEN HAVE you cast your fly numerous times, only to check it and find there's nothing there? As my good friend Nonie would say, "I've been fishing on credit for the last half hour." Check your flies often to be sure they haven't snapped off and that you don't have a dangling piece of thread or moss. Perhaps you are somehow snarled into a rat's nest. The fish can spot these imperfections a mile away.

After hours of fishing on the Caney Fork River, Cindy Denham told me she had spent half of her time in a tangled mess. We spent a little time working on her cast to be sure she was fishing knot-free. Once the timing of her cast was back in rhythm, it didn't take long before she was netting fish.

Sometimes it's simply a matter of a few small adjustments to improve your fish-catching success rate. The next time you are having a challenging day, remember these tips and give them a try. I think you'll find your luck and spirits will change for the better.

CHAPTER 23

Flies That Catch Fish

OR THE PAST 15 years, I have looked forward each December to receiving my email from Sheila Hassan, director of the Wulff School. In this email, she asks the Wulff School instructors to select our available teaching dates for classes being held May through June the following year. Once my dates are selected, I count down the days until the time arrives.

I have loved every minute of my time teaching at the Wulff School, and it's extra special when friends or family can attend. Over the years, my sister, Cindy, attended the Trout Fishing class, my dad and mom received the grand tour, and then, to top it off, several of the Music City Fly Girls attended. It makes me so proud to have each of them join in and experience, firsthand, what I have been enjoying for 15 years.

On one particular weekend, Shan Raetzloff and Susan Henderson, longtime Music City Fly Girls members, attended the school. We decided to stay an additional day once the class ended so we could fish the Beaverkill River. We had a room at the Beaverkill Valley Inn, a quaint little spot where Wulff School students typically enjoy accommodations while they are in town for the class. Besides being within walking distance of the school and having a great lobby, cozy fireplace,

MY FAMILY AT THE WULFF FISHING SCHOOL

MUSIC CITY FLY GIRLS AT THE BEAVERKILL VALLEY INN ON THEIR WAY TO CASTING SCHOOL

and delicious food, another great advantage of being at the inn is access to 2 miles of private water located just steps from the front door.

We were at breakfast one morning planning our fishing day when a friendly gentleman introduced himself to the three of us and asked if he could take photographs while we were fishing. Walter Hodges, a professional photographer, explained that he was working with the inn and updating their brochure and website. He was hoping for some stream-side shots. Of course, we eagerly said yes. Who wouldn't want to be a fly fishing model!

SUSAN (LEFT) AND SHAN (RIGHT) WITH JOAN WULFF AT WULFF'S TROUT FISHING SCHOOL

Susan, Shan, and I rigged our gear and, without hesitation, I put on one of my favorite Catskills "confidence flies," the Royal Wulff. This is one of Lee Wulff's original dry fly creations and is a well-known, classic pattern. It seemed fitting to select this fly, considering our surroundings.

We ventured into the water that morning, and our photographer was situ-

THE ROYAL WULFF FLY

ated up on the rock wall directly across from us. As good fortune would have it, I cast my fly in a spot that had a hungry rainbow trout just lying in wait. The photo was snapped the moment the fly was

JUST THE RIGHT TIME, JUST THE RIGHT PLACE, JUST THE RIGHT FLY
Photographed by Walter Hodges for the Beaverkill Valley Inn

taken. What a treat! We all went on to catch several more fish that day, but this one certainly sticks out in my mind.

I'm a big believer in confidence flies. I define these as your own personal favorite patterns with which you have had countless days of success. These may not be the flies recommended by fly shops or other guides, but your gut tells you that you will catch fish if you stick with your lucky patterns.

I can't tell you how many times I've traveled to fish new water and stopped in at the local fly shop prior to heading out to fish. Of course I always ask, "What flies are working?" Often, the fly shop will recommend the hot, local patterns. I know many of you are nodding your head in agreement, fully understanding how easy it is to leave the shop with $40 worth of the newly recommended patterns. However, the story always ends the same way. Without fail, I start out with the new flies, and then somehow, before I even realize it, I'm falling back on my confidence flies and catching fish. And with that, another set of unused flies goes into the fly storage bin. Sound familiar?

Before I tell you about my own personal favorites, let's take a look at the different categories of flies and their characteristics. Once you read through this chapter, you may find it helpful to go back and read Chapter 3 again. The different stages of the insects and their imitations will begin to make sense the more you see them side by side, and after a while you will quickly be able to categorize these patterns.

Fly-Imitation Categories

I F YOU GO to a river to fish for the first time and have no idea what the fish may be feeding on, you may find this filtering type of approach helpful in keying in on the fly that will be most productive. You will first start with casting a very wide net, so to speak, and then step down until you find just the right pattern.

- **SEARCHING PATTERNS** This fly imitates as many bugs as possible, or casts the widest net. It's used to find fish and determine feeding patterns so you can close in on the color, size, and insect profile the fish are favoring. This fly can also help in determining where the fish are feeding in the water column. Materials used are somewhat wiry or messy and typically have muted colors. Examples of a searching pattern would be a hare's ear, prince nymph, or Parachute Adams. Some searching patterns will also fall into the attractor category, and vice versa.

- **IMPRESSIONISTIC PATTERNS** Once the fish are located, you can select a fly that's more specific to the actual insect the fish are focusing in on. The impressionistic fly will give a distinct illusion of a natural insect and represents a more narrow range of insect types. For example, the shape and silhouette will be captured with this type of fly. Examples of impressionistic patterns would include pheasant tails, Copper Johns, or Elk Hair Caddis.

- **IMITATIVE (REALISTIC) PATTERNS** This fly matches the main insect the fish are after, skillfully representing the size, color, and profile of a specific species. It will have such a remarkable resemblance to the natural insect, you will think it is the real thing. Examples of an imitative fly would be a Pat's Rubber Legs, zebra midge, yellow sally, blue wing olive, pale morning dun, and Shark's caddis larva.

Attractor Patterns

This pattern doesn't fit into the filtering system above. It's a fly that is used to entice a fish but doesn't replicate an insect found in nature. In many cases, the attractor will have unnatural coloring such as pink or purple. Often, the fish will attack this fly just because they are curious or because it's so flamboyant they can't help themselves. Examples of an attractor would be a Rainbow Warrior, Eat at Chucks, Chernobyl Ant, and Royal Wulff.

My Personal Favorites

THESE ARE FLIES that I always have with me whether I'm fishing my own home waters or waters in other areas of the country. I have great confidence in them; however, I believe success is more about how you fish a fly than the fly itself. That said, I'm certain there's a little magic in each of these flies, which adds to the success equation.

• **THRASHER'S MAGIC MIDGE** This is one of the simplest flies imaginable. In fact, if you've ever had any interest in fly tying, this one would be a great fly to start with (for instructions, see page 247). It has four components; a size 14 scud hook, black thread, a silver tungsten bead, and a little Thrasher magic. I believe the slender profile is the key characteristic of this fly. I consider it to be an impressionistic pattern, as it can replicate a small leech, black fly larva, midge larva, or snail. I've tied dozens of these for folks but don't have the time anymore to tie this commercially. If you are interested in trying them out, check with Doug Benson at Northwest Flies (greatflies.com).

GARDNER'S NEVER BUG

• **GARDNER'S NEVER BUG** I first learned about this fly through an Internet search. I was trying to find a searching pattern that would get down deep quickly. This one in particular caught my eye because of its "bugginess." It's also a fun fly to tie. I have had success fishing the Never Bug deep, bouncing along the bottom, and I've also found that it works well on the swing. As it rises up through the water column to the surface, the partridge collar gives it the appearance of an emerging insect.

- **PAT'S RUBBER LEGS STONE FLY** This fly is a great example of an imitative fly. It not only fools fish but has fooled me as well. I left one on the dining room table one day, and when I saw it a few days later, I picked up a

PAT'S RUBBER LEGS STONE FLY

magazine to give it a good swat before realizing my mistake. The rubber legs give it great motion in the water. If you are fishing in waters with an abundance of stone flies, you need this.

- **FRENCHIE** I absolutely love this attractor. I love how it looks in my fly box, I love tying it, and I love that the fish can't leave it alone. It's basically a fancy bead-head pheasant-tail nymph with a pink hot spot. I've had great success with the size 14.

FRENCHIE

- **EAT AT CHUCK'S** My friend Chuck Robinson created this attractor. Before he moved to Seattle, Chuck had a great fly shop in Nashville called the Fly Chucker. This pattern has been used all over our Middle Tennessee tailwaters. Thanks, Chuck, for leaving a lasting mark on Nashville. I swing these little guys every season.

EAT AT CHUCK'S SOFT-HACKLE FLY

- **NEVERSINK CADDIS** This is one of my absolute favorite dry flies. I make it a point to tie a bunch of these before fishing in the Smoky Mountains. The yellow foam body makes it extremely buoyant and very easy to follow as it moves through the plunge pools of the mountain streams. This attractor will imitate both caddis flies and yellow stone flies.

NEVERSINK CADDIS

- **MOP FLY** I'm sure many folks will scoff at this fly being in my list of favorites, but I have used this fly on both cold- and warm-water rivers and lakes and have caught trout, bream, carp, catfish, crappie, and bass. Tied on larger hooks like a size 4, they tend to resemble a threadfin shad. Smaller sizes can imitate scuds and crane fly larva. When tied in green, they look similar to the green inchworm. Perhaps the disrespect for them comes from the fact that they are tied using bathroom rugs or microfiber cleaning mitts. Whatever the reason, I encourage you to give these killer flies a try.

MOP FLY

All these flies have proven themselves time and again. I use them with clients on guided trips where the pressure is on and I'm determined to help people catch fish. Try them—they may become your confidence flies too.

CHAPTER 24

Photographing
Your Catch

HAVE HUNDREDS OF pictures of fish that I've caught over the years. Believe it or not, as I flip through the photos, I can remember unbelievable details about each fishing trip. Details such as who I was with, what flies I was using, the location, and the weather easily come to mind. That's why I'm a big believer in taking photos, so that with just a glance, it will take me right back to that place and time.

There are times that, with or without pictures, the sounds, smells, and emotions of a moment can all come rushing back like a warm wave of joy. This is exactly what it's like when I think about the Music City Fly Girls trip to Glenwood Falls in Colorado. This would be Nikki's final trip with the Fly Girls, and we savored every moment.

We boarded Amtrak's *California Zephyr* for the 6-hour train ride along the Colorado River on our way to Glenwood Springs. We booked our seats in coach this time since we weren't staying overnight on the train. Once we left the station, we headed back to the observation car, where we spent the majority of our time. Elaine and Nikki broke out

MUSIC CITY FLY GIRLS AT THE DENVER STATION ABOUT TO BOARD THE TRAIN

their watercolors, and the rest of us sat around and told stories, visited, and watched the amazing scenery.

During our time in the observation car, the conductor told us to keep a close eye on the Colorado River whenever we saw the whitewater rafters floating by. The river was nicknamed "Moon River," he said. We wondered why, but our questions were answered within a few minutes when a boatload of rafters waved as they saw the train approaching. As the observation car passed by the rafters, they all turned around with their backsides facing us and yanked down their pants.

We pulled into the Glenwood Springs station early that afternoon and made our way across the pedestrian bridge to the Hotel Glenwood Springs. From the bridge, we could see the famous hot springs, and we would definitely be taking a dip in those before the trip was over.

Over the next few days, we fished the Colorado River, the Roaring Fork, and the Frying Pan. As with all of our trips, some of the club members preferred fishing a day and sightseeing a day, so half of the group took the shuttle to Aspen for a quick tour, lunch, and a little shopping. This last trip with Nikki was an amazing time. The weather was picture-perfect, the train was right on time, the fishing included catching, and we flew home filled with even more love for one another.

When the details of special moments are seared into your mind, photos aren't really necessary, but it's sure nice to have them. One of the best things about taking fish pictures is that the primary subject, the fish, is an amazing work of art. If you aren't careful, you can ruin the shot simply by the way you hold the fish. Even worse, you can harm the fish if you aren't mindful of several factors. Let's go through a few things to remember when getting that great "grip and grin" shot.

Protecting the Fish

REMEMBER MY FRIEND Juni Fisher telling our local Trout Unlimited chapter about the importance of carefully handling a trout. She said,

"Trout aren't like catfish. With a catfish, you can stand on the dock and take several pictures, throw it in the trunk of the car and take it home, put it in the bathtub for the kids to play with, take a few more pictures, then throw it back in the river, and it will swim away, no worse for the wear." It's definitely not the same with trout. They are delicate creatures and must be handled gently.

Be mindful of the amount of time the fish is out of the water. A good rule of thumb is to hold your breath once you carefully lift it from the water. When you run out of air, it's time to put them back in; most likely, they will be out of air also.

When you place them back in the water, do so with ease. Cradle your hand softly around them under the water until you feel them swim out of your hand. You don't want to toss them in the water with a plop. Trout don't like belly flops. Show some respect and release them with grace.

The Snapshot

D O NOT, UNDER any circumstance, lip a trout as you would a bass. That means sticking your thumb inside its mouth and pinching the lower lip for the picture. You could seriously hurt or even kill the fish.

When holding the fish for the picture, be mindful of where you place your hands. I've seen so many pictures with just the head and tail of the fish showing and all the marvelous spots hidden behind fat fingers. The best shot can be captured by holding the fish with your fingers under the belly or simply holding the fish with one hand so that a good portion of it is exposed. Do not squeeze the fish or put any amount of pressure on the belly. If it struggles, let it go, or you will risk serious damage to the fish. You will have a chance for another picture with other fish. If you keep trying to get the perfect shot, the fish could die if it's put under too much stress.

LYNN GRAHAM HAD THE BIG FISH OF THE TRIP WITH THIS BEAUTIFUL BROWN.

LEANN KOLEAS WITH A BEAUTIFUL RAINBOW FROM THE OBEY RIVER

Avoid shoving the fish toward the camera with your arms out-stretched. Sure, it might make the fish look bigger, but your hands will look gigantic, and you won't be fooling anyone.

Having the fish in the net or very close to the water is ideal since you won't run the risk of harming the fish. Even better, use an over-under lens on your GoPro. An underwater shot of the fish still hooked or in the net can be very eye-catching as well.

Timing

HAVE YOUR CAMERA HANDY. There's nothing worse than getting the fish of a lifetime and, just when it's time for the picture, remembering your camera is located at the bottom of a dry bag. I usually keep mine in the pocket of my vest or pack for easy access. Even if you are fishing alone, you can get some great shots. Try lifting the fish from the net with one hand and taking a quick shot with the other. Or you can quickly set your camera on a rock after the fish is netted and still in the water. I use my Apple Watch camera app as a remote control to take self-timer shots. It works great. However, as Fly Girl Leann Koleas is demonstrating, sometimes it takes two hands!

The bottom line with the photos is to set a higher priority on the health of the fish than the quality of the photo. There's nothing more heartbreaking on the river than seeing a fish turn belly up. Keeping just a few of these simple things in mind will ensure the fish are protected and will give you a chance at some excellent bragging shots.

CHAPTER 25

Knowing How the Fish Are Feeding

Not long after we lost Nikki, another Montana, Music City Fly Girls trip was planned. Nikki loved Montana and wanted her ashes placed in a beautiful river somewhere in that vast, Big Sky State. Rhonda, her dear friend from the Russian flight adventure, was headed to Montana during the same time as the Fly Girls but to a different part of the state where she and Nikki had visited years before. She had plans to memorialize Nikki in her own special way, so we agreed to place her ashes in two different rivers. As the Music City Fly Girls and Rhonda left from Nashville, each heading our separate ways, we all had Nikki with us.

We decided to have our small service for Nikki on a crisp September morning beside the Madison River. As we gathered streamside, each preparing to share our favorite Nikki story, I walked with Nikki's ashes into the center of the river. Through tears, we each shared our memory. When the time came to release Nikki's ashes, thousands of white trico mayflies began to hatch all around us. Tricos are the tiniest of mayflies and resemble little white feathers. The sky was filled with them, glistening in the sun. It still gives me goose bumps as I remember this so

THE MUSIC CITY FLY GIRLS ON THE MADISON RIVER JUST BEFORE THE HATCH OF HATCHES

vividly. As you may remember from previous chapters, Nikki's life trail marker seemed to be a white feather, and she spoke of these often. It truly seemed she was with us in spirit on the water that day.

Since then, during special moments on the river, I've had a number of white feather days. On one particular day, I was guiding Mary Osborne, a client visiting from Iowa, and we were floating in my tandem Jackson Big Tuna kayak on the Elk River. Earlier in the day when we launched, I spotted a white feather and told her the Nikki story.

With fly fishing, some days it's more about fishing than catching. On this day, it was all about catching. Midway through the day, after landing a boatload of fish, another white feather floated by. This wasn't a small duck feather like the one we had spotted earlier. This white feather was gigantic, like the size you would see used as an old-fashioned pen quill. As it floated by, Mary said, "Look, another Nikki sign, signaling an amazing time on the water today." I chuckled and agreed. However, at that moment, I wondered if I was putting too much stock in this white feather business. Perhaps it was all coincidence and seeing white feathers was just because I was so aware of them, making it only natural that I could spot them anytime they were around. No sooner had this doubting thought gone through my mind than a trout came up forcefully out of the water and gobbled up that enormous white feather. I've never doubted it again!

Sometimes trout do actually break the surface when feeding, and it's easy to see what they are feeding on. Other times it's a little more subtle. Let's take a look at the types of movement on the water that may help in determining how the fish are feeding.

Trout Rise Forms

• **THE RING** The circular rise form, which results in rings forming on the surface, is the rise that gets all fly fishers' hearts pounding. The fish are slowly coming to the surface and taking flies off the top of the water. If you see multiple rises, look on the surface or in the air to see what may be hatching, and then select a fly of a similar size. Often I'll select a fly that's a little larger than the natural insect. My logic behind this is that with hundreds of flies passing by, why not select the "Big Mac"? It's worked for me many times.

● **THE DIMPLE** The small disturbances on the surface, which resemble tiny dots rather than a large ring, could signify trout taking insects that are hung up in the surface film. These could be dying insects such as spent spinners or pupae that were unable to break through to the surface.

● **THE SPLASHY TAKE** Sometimes you will hear a fish breaking the surface while feeding. This will resemble the ring rise but with a splash. This could indicate that the fish are keying in on caddis flies. The caddis will often skate across the water, causing the fish to go crazy. If you see this happening, try tying on a caddis fly. You may want to experiment with a slow drift and then change it to make the fly skip or jump on the water. Then you better hold on tight!

● **TAILING FISH** If you see the tail of a fish moving above the water, you will know they are foraging for nymphs, larvae, and crustaceans in the weed beds or off the bottom of the river. This typically occurs in shallow water. Watch closely, because at first glance, it may be mistaken for a rise to the surface for a dry fly. However, if you can get close enough, you may see the tail above water for several seconds at a time. This is a sure sign of how the fish is feeding and is a dead giveaway to use a subsurface fly to entice them. An effective technique could be a dry-dropper setup. You would have a dry fly, which would serve as your strike indicator, with a nymph dropped below. Since it's shallow water, the tippet tied to the bend of the dry-fly hook may only need to be 6–12 inches in length.

- **SWIRLS** This type of rise has fooled me many times. It appears the fish are taking dries, but looking closely, you will see the head does not emerge from the water. As the fish lunges forward to take flies from the surface film, the water moves similar to the typical "ring" rise. This swirl, or bulge, gives a clue that the trout are actually taking emergers just under the surface. This is a perfect time to swing a wet fly through the current.

- **BROKEN WATER** There are times you will see an unnatural disturbance at the surface. You won't see a ring formed or any part of the fish coming to the surface. It will be more like what you would see if you move your hand back and forth underwater. It's simply a break in the flow of the current. This could signal that a fish is diving to intercept nymphs or larvae that are moving in the water column. In this case, fishing nymphs under an indicator would be ideal.

When you reach the water to begin fishing, the tendency is to start casting right away. However, if you can be patient and watch the surface for a few minutes carefully, you may be able to find clues as to how the fish are feeding. Before too long, you won't be able to pass by a body of water without studying it closely. Even if I'm not fishing, I enjoy watching the water and just imagining what is going on beneath the surface.

CHAPTER 26

Fishing from a Kayak

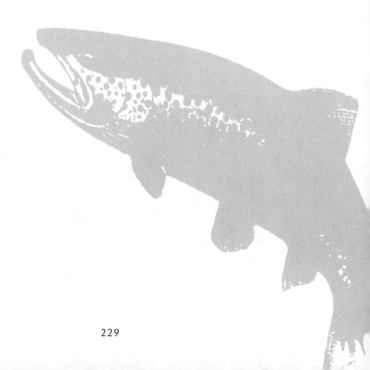

A FAVORITE OUTING FOR the Music City Fly Girls is a weekend trip to the Elk River. The Elk is a tailwater below Tims Ford Dam, located near Lynchburg, Tennessee, home of the Jack Daniels distillery.

During this outing, we decided to stay in Tullahoma at the Holiday Inn Express so we could spend two days fishing the river. The great thing about the club on these outings is the value in numbers. We have no problem bunking together, four to a room, to see the savings. This enables us to take many more trips since the cost of outings is so economical. On this weekend, Captain Chris and Shan were sharing a room. Chris is nicknamed "Captain" based on her flying days as a pilot in the Air Force and with Continental Airlines. She was up early enjoying the complimentary breakfast and had just returned to the room, where Shan was beginning to stir. When Shan asked Captain Chris to bring her a cup of coffee, Chris stated frankly, "Get it yourself, Scooter." Of course, Shan has been known as Scooter ever since.

We all joked and laughed about the new nickname as we loaded up our gear and secured the kayaks to our vehicles. We made a quick stop to see Rhonda Page at Tim's Flies and Lies to pick up our local hot flies, and then it was off to the river. There were a dozen of us headed

THE MUSIC CITY FLY GIRLS ON THE ELK RIVER

HOOKUPS ALL DAY LONG

off to fish, each with a kayak, and we couldn't wait to get started. For some reason we had a feeling that it was going to be a very productive day. Boy, did that premonition take shape.

Not long after we started the float, cheers started as one Fly Girl and then another began to hook and land fish. No sooner than a cast was made than another fish was in the net. This lasted the entire day. When we finally loaded up the boats and headed back to the hotel, we had netted around 250 fish. This was truly one of the most epic Fly Girls trips on the books.

One reason for our success was that we each had kayaks, which enabled us to access deep areas where the typical wade-fisherman was unable to go. On this particular day, it paid great dividends.

One of the things I enjoy sharing with beginners is that fly fishing is an activity that can be studied and built upon for a lifetime. Some beginners are surprised to hear that access to the water extends beyond simply wading into the river or stepping into a drift boat with a guide. Many are intrigued by the idea of fly fishing from a kayak. This is one of my favorite ways to fish, and if you haven't ventured out to try it, this chapter may help to pique your interest and provide you with some helpful tips.

Coordination

To some, FLY fishing from a kayak may seem intimidating and may appear to require more coordination than they are capable of producing. However, it just takes a little practice. One way to test this out is to sit on the ground and cast. All the essential casting rules and techniques apply; you're just starting your cast a little closer to the water. You'll need to practice line control and line management, and this comes with practice. For some, stripping in line and placing it in your lap works well. For others, allowing the fly line to float alongside the kayak is easier. The best way to find out what works for you is to get out and try it.

I typically lay my paddle across my lap once I reach a location where I want to cast. However, paddle holders may be mounted on the side of the kayak, which gets the paddle completely out of the way. Be sure to attach a leash to your paddle in case you drop it in the water.

KAYAK CLASS AT SOUTHERN BROOKIES WITH CO-INSTRUCTOR SAMANTHA CHRISTIAN

KAYAK CLASS IN THE POND BEFORE VENTURING TO THE RIVER

That way, you won't have to swim after it or have it swept away with the current. This was a lesson I learned the hard way: I was fishing on the Harpeth River on a fall day when, somehow, I let myself get caught in the current. I leaned over the wrong way, and before I knew it the boat flipped, and I was scrambling to grab my rod and other gear and swimming to shore. Fortunately, I had a rope tied to the front of the kayak so I could keep it from floating away, but the paddle was long gone. I waited on shore for an hour before someone in a canoe offered to tether me to their boat and float with me downstream. I never did find that paddle.

Outfitting Your Kayak

BASICALLY, YOU CAN fish out of anything that floats; however, I have found that a sit-on-top kayak (the type with no enclosure) or a stand-up paddleboard works best. It makes line management easier and gives you more room to move around and to access your gear. You also have room to pack extras such as rain gear, insect repellent, and sunscreen.

With the paddleboards, I secure a small cooler to the top of the board. It serves not only as a cooler but also as a seat and a place to

ANGELA PREPARES TO LAUNCH THE JACKSON BIG TUNA ON THE ELK RIVER.

balance yourself as you stand to cast. Paddleboards are very stable, and it's almost impossible to turn them over.

I'm a big fan of Jackson kayaks and paddleboards, and not just because they are made in Tennessee. They have a number of models, and many are specifically designed with the angler in mind. Check out the Superfishal, Coosa, Big Tuna, and Mayfly. I have used each

FILMING A SEGMENT FOR *TENNESSEE'S WILD SIDE* ON THE JACKSON STANDUP PADDLEBOARD WITH JOEY MONTELEONE

THE JACKSON SUPERFISHAL SETUP

Photographed by Nonie Sanders

of these and find them to be very well built, stable, and extremely durable.

Although you can buy kayaks designed for fishing that come outfitted with all of the accessories, you don't have to buy a new boat if you already have a standard kayak. It's easy to add the extras to make kayak fishing more enjoyable. I have listed below a few key accessories that I have found helpful.

• Small **kayak anchors** are ideal when you find a successful fishing spot and want to stay in one place. Either the current or the wind can move you out of position, and using an anchor will keep you from having to paddle back upstream.

• Mounting a **rod holder** within reach is also handy. This gets the rod out of the way when you are paddling between fishing areas. I have found Scotty fishing products to be ideal for outfitting my kayaks.

• Small **soft-sided coolers** are perfect for the kayak. You can secure your cooler with a carabiner or bungee cord, and they are just the right size for lunch, a few snacks, and a bottle of water.

• A **dry box** is strongly suggested to hold a set of keys, your phone, and a small camera. Nothing ruins a day faster than dropping your iPhone in the water! The box may be attached to your seat or the boat so it stays secure, and there is no risk of it floating away.

• Don't forget your **personal flotation device** (PFD). Not only are they a must for safety, but they are required on most rivers, and the fines can be steep if it's discovered that you don't have one on the boat with you.

Kayaking vs. Wading

ONE OF THE many advantages of fishing out of a kayak is the ability to float beyond the crowds. I have arrived early at river access points, only to find anglers standing shoulder to shoulder. When you are wading, you may be limited to the distance you can put between you and your fellow angler. In a kayak, you can quickly move beyond the access point and fish in less populated areas. Kayaking is so versatile. You can spend the full day floating and never leave the boat, or you can move between locations and step out of the kayak to wade into new areas.

Kayaking Etiquette

EVERYONE ON THE river is out to enjoy the day, so remember the Golden Rule. You wouldn't want someone walking through your fishing spot, so be polite to others. When approaching other anglers, bring in your line. If possible, paddle behind them, and avoid disturbing the water where they are fishing. If it's too shallow or impossible to move behind them, excuse yourself, and float quietly past them. The river is for everyone's enjoyment, so please be kind and respectful. Also, don't forget to pack out more than you take in. Unfortunately, we have people who use our rivers as garbage cans. It doesn't take much to pick up a discarded can or bottle that you see floating in the water or along the bank.

If you haven't tried fishing from a kayak, you should really give it a try. Pack a lunch and be ready for a relaxing day. Even on days when the fish don't cooperate, the float alone will be well worth the trip.

CHAPTER 27

Fly Tying

'VE NEVER BEEN one to enjoy crafts. I'm not a fan of sewing, scrapbooking, or knitting, and I find baby showers where you play games and make things to be among the most painful times one can experience. So you can imagine my mother's surprise when a fly-tying vise and all the materials were on my Christmas list one year. My parents generously placed a Renzetti vise, several bobbins of thread, feathers, hooks, and beads and a fantastic how-to book under the tree that year, and I couldn't wait to get started.

I was living in Virginia Beach when I started down the fly-tying path. Charlottesville was the closest place I could find to do any trout fishing. One weekend, I couldn't wait to get to the stream. I had spent the week before learning to tie a caddis fly. For a beginner, this fly is a little more complex since the deer or elk hair can be a little persnickety when trying to tie in the wing. My first attempts weren't going to win a prize, but they looked enough like the examples in my how-to book that I felt certain they would work. I was eager to give them a try.

I can still remember the exact spot where I was standing when I cast my newly tied elk-hair caddis upstream and watched it drift along in the current. The fly had only been on the water a few seconds when a trout rose to take the fly. Honestly, I could barely contain my excitement. I had caught a good share of trout since that first outing with my dad, but this catch was extra special. This was a trout caught on a fly that I had created myself. The experience that day added a whole new dimension to my fly fishing. I was completely hooked on fly tying.

Since then, I've tied countless flies. I'm not an expert by any means, but I can get the job done. All the flies I use when guiding, with a few exceptions, I tie myself. There's something satisfying about it. I know that other guides reading this chapter can relate to my experience of getting off the water with clients late in the afternoon and then needing to spend an hour or two at the tying bench that night in preparation for the next day. No matter how many flies I tie over the winter, I always seem to run short. It's part of the job, and I love it.

The opportunities for a beginning fly tier are much better now than when I started. Although the how-to book was helpful, I found YouTube videos to be beyond comparison. My favorite tutorials are by Tim Flagler of Tightline Productions (practicalpatterns.com). Tim has a very calming voice with step-by-step, easy-to-follow instructions. You can also check with your local fly shop about lessons. In Nashville, we have a full-service fly shop called Fly South. The owner, Jim Mauries, and Buckley Lewis, on staff, are master tiers. They offer classes to help beginner and advanced tiers. There's nothing like a hands-on tutorial.

Getting started can be somewhat confusing. It's easy to walk into the fly-tying section of a fly shop and be overwhelmed by the amount of feathers, thread, dubbing, and tools. However, there are a handful of items you can purchase to get you started. This chapter will focus on these items, along with a list of simple flies to start with. Then you can move on to a class or an online video for detailed instructions.

Vise

THIS IS ONE of the key tools you will need to get started. There are a number of options out there. You could go for something cheap but, keep in mind, you get what you pay for. Sometimes, on the cheaper vises, the jaws can slip or be difficult to adjust. There's nothing more frustrating than having the hook slip from the vise grip, causing your thread to break or materials to unravel. I suggest spending a little extra and getting a decent vise that will last. The Renzetti Traveler I received for Christmas has lasted 20 years and is in great shape. I'm sure there are other brands out there that are equally matched in design and durability. The Renzetti vise can be purchased with either a pedestal base or a C-clamp. I suggest the pedestal since you may be tying on a table where the C-clamp will not attach properly. This vise also breaks down, making it easy for traveling. You can expect to pay in the $200 range. *renzetti .com/traveler-series*

Tools

RENZETTI TRAVELER VISE

THERE ARE A few basic tools you will need to begin your fly tying. You will be able to tie dozens of patterns with these tools alone, and you can add to them as you progress to tying more-complex flies.

SCISSORS

BELIEVE IT OR not, there are a number of fly-tying scissors with varying blade shapes and angles for precise cuts. To start with, all you need is a pair of straight-edged scissors. Make sure they feel good in your hand and the holes are large enough to fit your fingers. A pair that I have used for a while are by Dr. Slick (Prism 4-inch model; drslick .com). The design was what initially caught my eye, but they aren't just good-looking. I have found them to be very durable and sharp as a razor as well. These are my go-to pair that I use on a weekly basis.

WHIP-FINISH TOOL

ONCE YOU WRAP the thread and feathers around the hook, you will need a way to tie off the thread. To do this, you can either use your

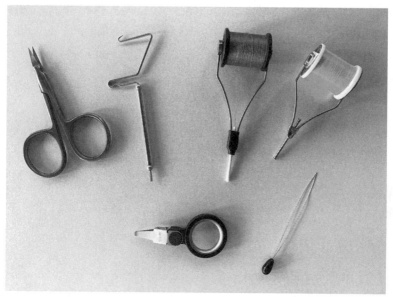

CLOCKWISE FROM TOP LEFT: SCISSORS, WHIP-FINISH TOOL, BOBBINS, THREADER, AND HACKLE PLIERS

fingers to tie a double half-hitch knot or use the whip-finish tool. The whip finish is by far the most durable knot. Some folks find using the tool confusing at first, but there are videos that show you how to do it. Watch a video in slow motion and practice over and over, and you will be able to pick it up quickly. I recommend learning to whip finish by hand also. If you ever misplace the tool, or you are traveling and happen to forget it, you will be able to finish off the fly even without the tool. Try to stick with it and power through the frustration of learning this. It's worth the effort, and it's a critical skill in fly tying.

Bobbin

The bobbin holds your spool of thread in place and allows you to keep the proper tension on the thread while tying. I have several bobbins so I can keep a number of colors of thread loaded and ready. However, you really only need one, and when you need to change colors, you just take out the spool and replace it. Wire loop tools are available for threading the bobbin; this tool makes it fast and easy, but it's not required.

HACKLE PLIERS

HACKLE PLIERS MAKE it easier to grab hold of the tip of a feather and wind it around the hook. You can do this with your fingers, but it's easy to lose your grip. Clipping the pliers to the tip enables a more secure hold.

Materials

ONCE YOU HAVE these tools in place, all you need are the materials. It's easy to go crazy with materials and start a collection that can quickly become unmanageable. I'm telling you this from my own personal experience. If you aren't careful, you will end up with tubs of unused material.

HOOKS

THE HOOK SERVES as the foundation of your fly, upon which everything is built. Hooks come in various sizes and shapes based on what the fly pattern is imitating. A number is used to indicate the size of the hook. The hook size relates to the gap between the point and the shank. The wider the gap, the larger the hook size. Typical fly patterns range in size from 2 to 18. Larger hooks are used for specialty flies. Once you get larger than a size 2, the hooks are labeled in ascending order using the aught system. For example, a "2/0" is referred to as a "2 aught" hook. The slash lets you know it's part of the aught system. Unless you are fishing with some monster-size flies, you will most likely be using hook sizes in the 4–18 range. Flies smaller than size 18 are used for micro-size

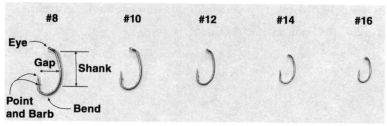

THE PARTS OF A HOOK AND VARIOUS HOOK SIZES

midges and mayflies. Learn to tie a few larger patterns before dropping down to this tiny fly. There are also different gauges, lengths, eyes, and shapes of hooks to consider, as defined below.

- **GAUGES** Use a lighter-gauge wire on dry-fly hooks to help them float, and a heavier gauge on streamers and nymph hooks to help them sink.

- **LENGTHS** Hooks are measured in standard lengths of "long" or "short." If the hook is above or below this standard, an X system is used to express this. For example, a hook that is "2X long" means that it is longer than standard, while a "2X short" means that it is shorter than standard.

- **EYES** Standard hook eyes can be straight, turned down, or turned up. You can use any style with any pattern. It really comes down to personal preference. I typically use straight eyes with my patterns. Jig-eye hooks are becoming more popular for nymphs and streamers. With these hooks the eye is turned down at either a 60- or 90-degree angle. When used with a slotted bead, the point is forced to ride up in the water, which helps eliminate snagging the bottom. This is something to consider if you are tying heavily weighted flies.

- **SHAPES** The shape of the hook will represent the size and body style of the fly pattern you are tying. For example, if you are tying a scud pattern, which resembles a small freshwater shrimp, the hook will have a curved shape. If you are tying a streamer pattern, resembling a baitfish, the hook will be long and straight.

THREAD

THREADS COME IN a variety of colors, materials, and diameters. The sizing can be a little confusing, so it's worth taking a look at how to read the spools. The number on the spool is not a standard system for all thread manufacturers. Some manufacturers use the aught system, and some use the denier system. The aught system refers to the thread diameter, and *denier* refers to the weight of the thread. In the aught system, the larger the number, the thinner the diameter. So, a spool labeled "3/0" would be thicker than one labeled "6/0." *Denier* is defined as the mass in grams of 9,000 meters of thread. A spool marked "70 denier" is lighter than a spool marked "210 denier." Regardless of the measurement used, a good rule of thumb is to use a thinner or lighter thread for small flies and a thicker or heavier thread for larger

flies. Thread can also be purchased waxed or unwaxed. I prefer waxed. It seems to hold better, it's easier when adding dubbing (see Glossary), and it won't cut into delicate material.

VARIOUS THREAD SIZES

BASIC GUIDE FOR THREAD SELECTION	
8/0 or 70 Denier	Small dry flies, midges, nymphs
6/0 or 140 Denier	Larger dry flies, nymphs, streamers
3/0 or 210 Denier	Salt water flies, bass bugs, large streamers

WIRE

WITH SOME PATTERNS, you will want to use wire on your flies. If trying to weight the fly, you will use a lead-wire wrap that will serve as the underbody. Once wrapped on the hook, it will be covered with thread and other materials and will be out of sight.

Wire used as part of the pattern will serve as a ribbing, giving the pattern a segmented look. The wire comes in small, medium, and large sizes depending on the size of your fly. The sizing varies across manufacturers, so experiment until you find what you like.

BEADS

BEADS CAN SERVE a number of purposes, such as adding flash (shine), adding weight, or imitating an air bubble. Using a bead for added weight will help the fly drop down into the current quickly. Some fly tiers prefer using beads over using a lead wrap (discussed above). Depending on how much weight you need, beads and lead wraps are used together. Beads come in different materials, such as glass, brass, and tungsten. Tungsten beads are the heaviest and cost a bit more, but they are worth it. You won't need to add as much weight to your tippet, and the flies will reach depth quickly. The sizing can be confusing; the bead sizes are typically given in inches or millimeters and should be selected based on the hook size you are using. If it's too small, the bead won't go around the hook bend. If it's too large, it will slide over the hook eye. Typically the package will state the hook-size range the bead will work with. Beads come with a hole in each end. Be careful to insert the hook point into the smaller hole so that the bead will be positioned correctly on the hook.

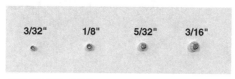

VARIOUS BEAD SIZES

Four Basic Flies

SUGGEST STARTING WITH these simple flies. This will allow you to keep the initial purchase to a minimum yet still tie some productive flies. You'll need the following materials.

MATERIALS LIST

- 2 Scud hooks, size 14
- Standard dry-fly hook, size 18
- Medium-size black chenille
- Small silver wire
- Silver tungsten beads (3/32" and 5/32")
- Strung peacock herl
- Black marabou feather
- Black 8/0 or 70-denier thread
- Streamer hook, size 8 (4X Long)
- Grizzly hackle

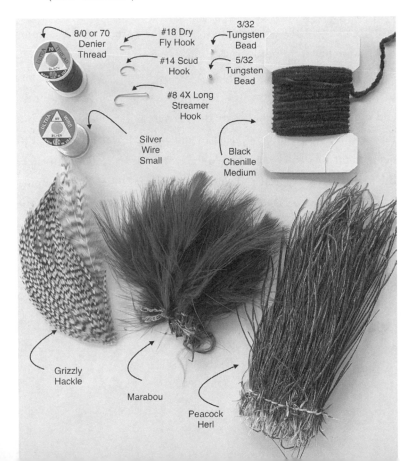

Thrasher's Magic Midge

- Hook: Scud, size 14
- Weight: Tungsten bead 3/32"
- Thread: Black 8/0
- Body: Black 8/0 thread

MAGIC MIDGE

Zebra Midge

- Hook: Scud, size 14
- Weight: Tungsten bead 3/32"
- Thread: Black 8/0
- Body: Black 8/0 thread
- Rib: Small silver wire

ZEBRA MIDGE

Woolly Bugger

- Hook: Streamer, size 8 (4X Long)
- Bead: Silver tungsten, size 5/32"
- Thread: Black 8/0
- Body: Medium black chenille
- Tail: Black marabou feather
- Hackle: Grizzly

WOOLLY BUGGER

Griffith's Gnat

- Hook: Standard dry fly, size 18
- Thread: Black 8/0
- Body: Strung peacock herl
- Hackle: Grizzly

GRIFFITH'S GNAT

Keep in mind, there are many excellent fly tiers out there, so don't feel compelled to stick with my recipes. In fact, I encourage you to listen and watch as many fly tiers as you can. There are different techniques and opinions, and the more you watch, the more you will learn.

As you begin to add to your fly-tying materials collection, try to keep it simple and organized. I picked up a few plastic storage cases from the hobby shop and found they worked perfectly for keeping hooks and beads separated and easy to transport. I used a permanent marker to label the boxes so I could easily pick out the needed hooks and beads. You may also want to check out fly-tying cases and pouches. Fishpond has a great fly-tying case that will keep thread, tools, and materials organized (fishpondusa.com). It's handy for travel and keeps your fly-tying gear all in one place.

As with anything, it will take a little practice to get the hang of it. Once you spend 30 minutes making a fly, you may find yourself climbing a tree to rescue it instead of just breaking it off. However, with practice, you will get faster and whip out a dozen in no time. The bottom line is this: there is tremendous satisfaction in catching fish using your own creation, and that is hard to beat.

CHAPTER 28

Packing for a Fly Fishing Trip

THE MUSIC CITY FLY GIRLS AT CROWLEY LAKE

I'LL NEVER FORGET the day Jeremy Hale called me and said his mom needed some fly fishing friends. He had heard about the Music City Fly Girls and hoped that she would join us. I gave him all the club information and promised to reach out to his mom and invite her to join. As we ended the conversation, he said, "Please take care of my Momma." Well, we have certainly tried to take care of Charley, but actually, she does a great job of taking care of us!

A few years ago, Charley suggested that we plan one of our Music City Fly Girls trips to the High Sierras. It turned out to be one of my all-time favorite group trips. Jeremy offered to guide us since he lives close to the area and fishes it quite often. We rented a couple of cabins at Crowley Lake and boarded our flight to

A BEAUTIFUL BROOK TROUT, ONE OF MANY CAUGHT THAT DAY

California. Once we arrived, we piled into our rented van and headed out for the 5-hour drive to trout waters.

We had a great time fishing on Crowley Lake, Hot Creek, and the Owens River, but the highlight by far was our time on Rock Creek. We spent the day hiking the trail along the creek and fishing the beautiful mountain stream. At one point, the creek opened up into a small lake known as the Pond, where snowpack runoff had formed a beautiful waterfall. We ventured into the water and began catching the most beautiful brookies with almost every cast. There were lots of woo-hoos and laughs as we spent the remainder of the afternoon enjoying the bite. The water was frigid and, at one point, I looked over at Marjorie and her teeth were chattering, but she wasn't about to miss this opportunity. We stayed on the creek until sunset and then made our way down the mountain for dinner at Tom's Place, a cozy little restaurant just a short drive from Rock Creek. We had a wonderful time enjoying a delicious dinner and reliving the fish stories from the day.

The trip was a great success, and Jeremy, along with his son Charlie and friends Jerry and Rich, was the perfect host. However, the biggest challenge for us was packing for the trip knowing we were limited on space due to flying and also traveling in a tightly packed rental van. We managed to make it work because the group followed a few packing suggestions.

Here are a few packing ideas to consider the next time you take a fly fishing vacation.

Luggage

SOFT-SIDED TRAVEL DUFFELS seem to work best when squishing and mashing them into tight spaces. When packing, I typically roll my clothes instead of folding them. It's amazing how tight you can pack

THE POND ABOVE ROCK CREEK

with this approach, and the clothes don't wrinkle like you think they
would. Plus, you are going fishing, so a few wrinkles won't matter.

Clothing

HOW MANY TIMES have you packed 10 sets of clothes for a three-
day trip only to wear the same things and take home many outfits
that weren't even touched? Consider rewearing clothes two or three

times. Remember, you are there to fish, and they don't care how fancy you look, so make it easy on yourself. Quick-dry slacks, shorts, and shirts are very thin and won't take up the space that bulky jeans or other cotton items will.

Outerwear

REGARDLESS OF THE season, I always take a packable puff jacket. It doubles as a rain jacket and helps with a chilly airplane, over-air-conditioned restaurants, and cool days on the water. Puff jackets are great because they pack down small enough to be zipped inside their own pocket. Most come with a loop so you can attach a small carabiner and snap it to your duffel.

Waders

MANY COMPANIES ARE coming out with packable waders and boots that fold up nice and tight and will fit in a midsize duffel with your other gear. If you know that you will be wading in small streams, you might even consider hip waders. Also, if you will be fishing from a drift boat, you may not even need to pack your waders. Ask your guide, and they can confirm this with you. Leaving waders behind can save a ton of space. However, if you do take them, be sure to pack a trash bag. If you plan to fish the day of your departure, you will want to wrap your boots in the trash bag to keep from getting everything else in your bag wet.

Rods

IF I'M FLYING, I never check a fly rod. Most of the rods I own are either four- or five-piece rods in a rod tube that can be easily strapped to my duffel. If you are fishing with a guide, you may even want to leave the rod behind. There have been times that it made more sense for me to leave my gear behind and use the guide's equipment. Ask your guides what equipment they use with clients. It may be a rod you've been hoping to try out anyway.

Gear

YOU CAN PACK your reel, fly fishing vest, lanyard, or pack in your duffel. Carefully consider what you will really need. If you are like me, you have stuff in your pack that you never, ever use. This is a good time to clean it out and pare it down to just the essential items. If you are carrying on your bag, be sure to know what is allowed through security. I mistakenly packed a small fly-tying case with scissors, bobbins, and other suspicious-looking items. The TSA agents let me through, but not until they fully inspected each and every item. They were not smiling when they motioned that I was free to go on to my gate. This was an embarrassing lesson learned.

Yard Sale or Thrift Store

I CAN'T CLAIM THE genius behind this idea but instead give full credit to Fly Girls Shan Raetzloff and Susan Henderson. The two of them flew out a week early on one of our Music City Fly Girls Montana trips, hoping to travel around and fish a few rivers before settling in with us. Since they were flying and didn't have room to pack a cooler, cooking utensils, and other items, they stopped by a few yard sales to pick up gear for a few dollars. Once finished, they dropped off the collection at Goodwill. This is an idea to consider if you will be going on an extended trip and need extra gear that's too difficult to transport.

CHAPTER 29

Tenkara Fishing

HAD A CLIENT recently who booked a multiday trip with me on the Caney Fork River. Greg Jowaisas and his brother, Dennis, came down from Kentucky and were wonderful guests. I especially enjoyed Greg's banjo picking around the campfire each night. This was the first time I had paid much attention to the banjo, and I fell in love with the clawhammer style and sound. Greg noticed my intense interest and offered to swap a banjo lesson for a lesson in double-haul fly casting at the pond. Of course, I jumped on the deal.

He taught me the basic technique and one song to practice. The picking seemed awkward at first, and my fingers didn't want to move like my brain was telling them to. Since Greg was coming back for another guided trip the following month, he offered to leave the banjo with me so I could practice. This was a very generous gesture, and I took full advantage of having this fine instrument. I practiced each day until he returned. After hours of practice, my fingers finally began to listen to my brain. I was finally getting it! Greg listened as I performed what he had patiently taught me, and I was thrilled to hear that he thought I had potential. It wasn't too long before I was purchasing my own banjo. Since then, I've been practicing religiously using You-

Tube videos and a banjo songbook that Greg put together for me. I've learned to play a dozen songs over the last nine months. I can't seem to get enough. So, as I was preparing for a long trip with the family, the thought of being away from my banjo for that long made me anxious.

PRACTICING MY TRANJO ON THE TRAIN TRIP TO SEATTLE

As I've mentioned before, I absolutely love train travel. I've been on several Amtrak trips with my family and the Music City Fly Girls. As another trip was quickly approaching, and as I was packing for the cross-country, 10-day train adventure with my parents and sister, I tried to think how I could incorporate some banjo practice. Only 24 hours before leaving on the journey, I began an Internet search to see if there was a traveling banjo on the market. To my surprise, not only were they available, but the creator of one of the best travel instruments around was located a short drive away in Franklin, Tennessee. Best of all, he happened to have one available that he could set up and have me plucking that afternoon. I can hear Debra now, saying, "You definitely live in the zone!"

I met Sam Farris, creator of the Tranjo (tranjo.com), in his workshop, and within an hour I was the proud owner of a traveling banjo.
I had already picked out the song "Black Jack Grove" as the tune I would try to learn while traveling. It turned out to be ideal!

What does the traveling banjo have to do with fly fishing? If you are anything like me, when you find something that you are passionate about, it's hard to leave it behind. That's where the traveling fly rod comes into the picture.

Meet the Tenkara

T ENKARA MEANS "FROM HEAVEN" in Japanese. This is fitting in my opinion. It is a very old traditional Japanese approach to fly fishing using only a rod, a line, and a fly. There is no reel involved. It

TENKARA BY TEMPLE FORK OUTFITTERS
(TFORODS.COM/TENKARA-FLY-RODS)

is the ultimate minimalist approach. Although the art of tenkara dates back several hundred years, it has become popular in the US just within the last 8–10 years.

The Setup

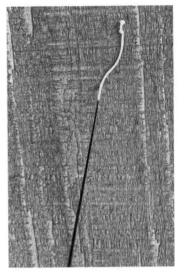

THE LILLIAN IS THE SHORT PIECE OF CORD AT THE TIP OF THE ROD WHERE THE LEADER IS ATTACHED.

HISTORICALLY, TENKARA RODS were made of bamboo, but today most are made with carbon fiber. They are long, lightweight, and very flexible, and lengths typically range from 10 to 14 feet. The cork grips are similar to those of regular fly rods, but the rod is telescoping, meaning that the sections collapse to a size of 18–20 inches. At the end of the rod, a short piece of cord, called a lillian, is glued to the tip. The line or leader is then attached to the lillian.

Unless you are a tenkara purist, there are no hard-and-fast rules to the line that is used, and the line setup is personal preference. The line can either be a tapered, furled leader (the traditional approach) or a level (all one diameter) section of line. The furled leaders are made up of twisted or braided thread or monofilament. The level lines are typically a single strand of monofilament or fluorocarbon. A short (3- to 4-foot) section of tippet is then attached to the line or leader. Typically, the length of the line plus the tippet is equal to at least the length of the rod, but is often much longer.

In addition to the lines described above, there is also a hybrid approach. This is the setup I tried with my first tenkara experience. The rod was rigged with a 20-foot section of thin, level running line (typical plastic-coated floating fly line). A tapered leader was attached, ending with a 5X tippet. This nontraditional tenkara setup has more of a traditional fly fishing feel to it. Again, the type of line used is a personal choice, so if you decide to give it a go, try the various options until you find what works best for you.

Flies

THE TRADITIONAL TENKARA fly is a wet fly tied with the hackles in a reverse position. However, this isn't the only fly pattern that will work. Unless you plan to stick with the traditional tenkara approach, all the typical patterns of dry fly, soft hackle, nymphs, and streamers may be used.

Landing the Fish

IF THE LINE length is equal to the length of the rod or greater, a hooked fish can be landed by simply lifting your arm high and sliding the fish into the net. If the line has been extended to a length longer than the rod, then the fish must be brought in by hand. This is done by gently lifting the rod until you can grab hold of the line and pull the fish in, sliding your hand down the leader to the fly and releasing the fish. Obviously, with the flexible rod and light tippet, some finesse is required, and if the fish is putting up a fight and moving downstream, you may need to run with him until he tires out before trying to bring him to the net. This just adds to the fun and the challenge.

Benefits

BECAUSE THE TENKARA rod collapses down in seconds to a very compact size, it is ideal for backpacking or hiking along mountain streams. The long rod aids in keeping line off the water and obtaining the perfect drifts. This is especially helpful in mountain streams with fast, tumbling currents. I have also found the tenkara to be a useful teaching tool. Beginners, especially children, can begin fishing immediately without the additional line and reel that needs to be tended. It's a great way to introduce them to casting in a short period of time.

I'll have to admit I was skeptical of this fishing method at first, but what truly caught my attention about tenkara was its simplicity. While I don't anticipate ever giving up my traditional fly fishing gear, there is a time and place for a tenkara rod. Just like my traveling banjo, I don't have to leave fly fishing behind when a hiking or camping adventure makes packing all the gear impractical. My friend Mary Elizabeth (M. E.) Sorci took hers along during her backpacking adventure along the Continental Divide Trail, which stretches from Mexico to Canada. Without it, she wouldn't have had the chance to catch fish in some of the most beautiful areas of the country.

One of the great things about fly fishing is the fact that there is always something new to learn, no matter how long you have been fishing or how advanced you've become. I've used my tenkara rods on both mountain streams and tailwaters with great success. Before scoffing at this idea, give it a try. It may add a little to your next outdoor travel adventure.

CHAPTER 30

Teaching Kids to Fly Fish

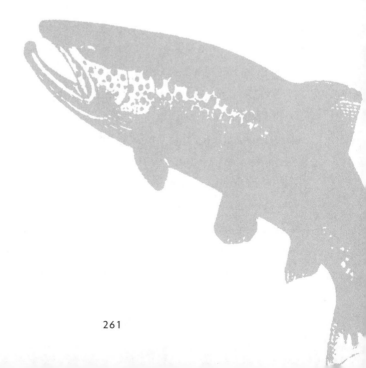

TRULY ADMIRE PARENTS and the time and patience they have with their kids. I don't have children of my own, but I'm lucky enough to have a wonderful nephew, Cody Ennis Jessee. As I write this, he is finishing college at Virginia Tech with a mining engineering degree and is planning to marry Sarah, his sweetheart. My sister and brother-in-law, Cindy and Russell, have done a fabulous job raising him, and I'm a superproud aunt of this fine young man.

CODY WITH HIS FIRST TROUT ON A FLY

When he was born, I couldn't wait to spoil him. I wanted him to hike, camp, mountain bike, kayak, and, of course, fly fish. For birthdays, Christmas, and any other holiday when I could find an excuse, I would load up on the gifts, from BB guns to fly rods. I couldn't wait until he was old enough to learn to cast. As with almost anything he tries, he picked it up quickly.

When he was 7, I took him on his first wade-fishing trip to the South Holston River. It was just a few hundred yards upstream of the spot where I had my first lesson. Cindy was with us, and we rigged our rods and waded out into the river. I had put on a large strike indicator and a bead-head pheasant tail for Cody. Cindy and I started to walk a little ways upstream to get out of his way and find our own fishing spots. We had only taken a few steps when I looked over to see Cody's rod bent double. He was holding it up tightly, and my first thought was that he was hung up on the bottom. Then I saw the look in his eyes and the thrill of joy on his face. It definitely wasn't the bottom!

Cody played the fish perfectly and, before too long, we had the beautiful trout in the net and were snapping pictures. I remember that day like it was yesterday. I was so proud of him.

These days, he spends more time trail running than fishing. In the summer of 2018, Cindy and I went with him to Colorado to watch as he ran in the 65-mile Never Summer trail race in Gould. We went early so that he could get acclimated to the altitude and, of course, to do a little fly fishing. He picked up his cast again quickly during that trip, and we spent several days fishing in some beautiful places.

Since those early lessons teaching Cody to cast, I've had the chance to introduce numerous other kids to fly fishing. I have learned a thing or two about what works and what doesn't. Below are a few tips that are sure to help during those initial days out on the water with your young fishing buddy.

What Age to Start

IN GENERAL, I don't recommend starting fly fishing with kids younger than age 7 or 8. Some kids could start younger, but in most cases, the kids aren't strong enough to hold the rod, and their attention span is very short.

Getting an Instructor

WHEN THEY ARE ready, it's a good idea to have someone other than a parent lead the instruction. It's important to have patience, and believe me, a kid will look around while you're talking, pick their nose, change the subject, ask "When will we be done?" or "Why are we doing this?" Leave the teaching to a professional. Both you and the child will benefit greatly from this choice. You can give it a try, but if either of you begins to get frustrated, consider going the instructor route. It will pay great dividends.

Where to Start

MOST CHILDREN WILL be unable to handle a rod with one hand, so I have found that teaching a two-handed method works well. Beginning with the roll cast, it is basically teaching half the cast. This is just enough to get them started. Once this is mastered, the backcast can be introduced. More on casting in Chapter 33.

Break It Up

DURING MY FULL-DAY outings with kids, I mix up the time we have together. We begin with a basic discussion on the gear so they know the difference between the fly line and leader. I typically go over how to hold the rod and the concept of casting the line, not the fly itself. Then we'll move on to casting using a yarn fly. It's a little dangerous to begin with a hook, so the hook doesn't come until a little later in the day. If at any time I see their eyes glaze over, I'll change it up by getting in the river with them and turning over rocks to look for bugs. I'm fortunate to have a casting pond for teaching, so I've also been known to have a kayak waiting on the bank. Letting them paddle around for a little while is also a way to break up the routine with something fun. It's important that the lesson doesn't feel like school. Otherwise, you will lose them.

Fly Tying

I ALSO LIKE TO incorporate tying a fly as part of the beginning fly fishing lesson when time allows. I will start with something simple like a San Juan Worm, simple Popper, or Woolly Bugger. Obviously, their first attempt may be a little rough-looking, but many times it will do the trick. If you can get a kid to lure in a fish on a fly that they have tied themselves, it's a sure bet they will be hooked.

Equipment

YOU WILL NEED a rod that will work with small hands and that is light enough for a child to handle without getting too worn out. As discussed in the previous chapter, a tenkara might be an excellent choice. Another of my favorites is a rod by Echo. This is a complete outfit including a 7'9" rod, reel, fly line, and case. It's offered in a 4/5 weight, is relatively lightweight for kids to hold, and has a small grip to fit smaller hands. I will often use this rod as a casting tool since the bright yellow rod is easy for students to follow. The complete package is under $200 and well worth the money.

Cold- or Warm-Water Fishing

REMEMBER THE PHRASE "the tug is the drug"? Starting a kid out on a fly rod by fishing in a pond or warm-water stream is an excellent way to get them off on the right foot. As we all know, trout are picky and often require precise, delicate casts; proper mends; and other advanced techniques. A child may have difficulty grasping this at an early age. That's why starting with fishing for bluegill on a fly rod is the perfect starting point. They don't spook as easily as trout; they attack the fly hard, and you can catch a ton of them. I personally love

ECHO'S FLY FISHING PACKAGE FOR KIDS, THE GECKO *Courtesy of Echo Fly Fishing (echoflyfishing.com)*

OLIVIA ON THE CANEY FORK RIVER *Photographed by John McMillan*

to fish for bluegill. They pull and fight much harder than you would expect for their size, so imagine the excitement of a child hooking a fish that fights like the devil! The bluegill is always my first choice for fishing with kids for this very reason.

Graduating to Trout

ONCE YOU ARE ready to step into the stream and focus on catching trout, be sure to outfit your youngster with a proper pair of waders. Trout water is cold, so keep them comfortable, warm, and dry. Safety is key, and you should either keep them very close or insist on a life jacket. As for flies, I like to begin with a wet fly or a nymph with a strike indicator. Swinging a wet fly in the current is a simple technique and enables the child to feel the fish strike. This is always exciting and tends to pique their interest once they feel the tug, even if they miss the first few hits. Using a nymph and a strike indicator works well because they most likely already understand the concept of fishing with a bobber. The next trick is to teach them to fish the fly with a proper drift. Just remember to use a strike indicator that is easy to see and keeps its buoyancy. It's hard to beat the joy of seeing the ear-to-ear grin on the face of a kid landing their first trout.

Again, each of these tips is a reminder that patience is key. Don't expect to keep kids on the river for an 8-hour day. Plan to incorporate a break for lunch, time for looking under rocks for bugs, or scouring the gravel bar for fossils. As happened with Cody, teaching a child at a young age to appreciate fly fishing will lead to a lifetime of memories and loving the outdoors.

CHAPTER 31

Casting for Recovery

As fly fishers, we all dream of making that long, graceful cast to a big brown we have seen sipping bugs off the top of the water. Presenting our handcrafted fly in just the right spot with the perfect drift is so rewarding, as we watch the trout rise and gulp down the fly, and then it's "Fish on!" My heart pounds just thinking about it! However, as rewarding as this is, I have found something that tops it all: Casting for Recovery.

Back in 2007, during the first Music City Fly Girls meeting, we all agreed that along with the fishing, we wanted to find an organization that we could volunteer our time to support. As good fortune would have it, we came upon Casting for Recovery (CfR), a national organization focused on breast cancer survivors. Several members of the Cumberland Chapter of Trout Unlimited and Wanda Taylor, who was the East Tennessee CfR retreat leader at that time, wanted to bring Casting for Recovery to Middle Tennessee. They needed volunteers and asked if we would be interested. It was a match made in heaven for our newly formed club. With no hesitation, we stepped right in to volunteer, and before we knew it we were quickly taking the lead.

Casting for Recovery is a nonprofit organization founded in 1996 in Manchester, Vermont. It provides weekend retreats across the country for women of any age and any stage of breast cancer treatment or recovery. The retreats are offered at no cost to the participants. The goals of these retreats are to offer a weekend free of the stress related to medical treatments, work, and general life pressures, and to teach the participants something new and challenging. Each retreat takes place in a beautiful setting with warm and caring volunteers. Along with fishing, the weekend provides the participants with support from trained facilitators, including a psychosocial facilitator, a health care professional, fly fishing instructors, and river helpers.

You may wonder what fly fishing has to do with breast cancer. Apart from the many benefits of being active in nature, the casting

THE HIGHLIGHT OF THE RETREAT IS SUNDAY ON THE RIVER.

motion can be therapeutic for increasing mobility in the arm and shoulder for women who have undergone surgery or radiation as part of their breast cancer treatment.

Each retreat, across the country, runs for 2½ days. In Middle Tennessee, the retreat is held at the Hinkle Hill Inn in Bell Buckle, Tennessee. Friday evening, when participants arrive, there is a group dinner, followed by an informal icebreaker to help participants and staff get to know one another. In Middle Tennessee, we do this around the campfire, and singer-songwriter Lori Ridgeway picks out some great, original tunes on her guitar. Someone might be joining in soon on the banjo! This is followed by a full day on Saturday of beginning fly fishing instruction, including a review of fly fishing gear and terminology, casting, knot tying, and even a session on fly tying. Each participant is outfitted with a preloaded fishing lanyard, rod and reel, and wading gear for their use throughout the weekend. The first day and a half, the retreat is staffed with female volunteers who provide an

GRUMPY IS ALWAYS A FAVORITE GUIDE. *Photographed by Lori Ridgeway*

intimate and personal setting to help the participants to share freely about their health experiences. We often find that many of the participants have never been part of a support group. This is the first opportunity many of the women have had to share their experience with others who have lived in their shoes.

The fly fishing instruction during this first day is all in preparation for the Sunday guided experience on the river. This grand finale is a focal point of the weekend: a day on the water with their own personal fly fishing guide. In the Middle Tennessee area, we are blessed with professional guides and anglers who generously volunteer to serve as guides for the retreat. David Perry of Southeastern Fly, my good friend and professional guide out of Nashville, organizes the guides for participants. He has never had a problem rounding up the 14 volunteers needed. In fact, he has a waiting list of backups in case someone has a conflict at the last minute.

Jeff Sweeney, the owner and operator of Arrowhead Ranch, generously donates access to his property, complete with stocked fishing lakes and a beautiful stretch of trout water along the Duck River. The area is perfect for wading, and the participants can access the water easily.

The day on the river is followed by a grand celebration, complete with a BBQ dinner, slide show memories of the day, a graduation ceremony, and, of course, some whopping fish stories. As participants pack up to leave, there is a sense that everyone is lingering, not really wanting to say goodbye to their newfound friends.

The Music City Fly Girls benefit in many ways from these weekend retreats as well. Not only do we have a chance to share in this heartwarming experience with our new friends, but we also have a number of participants who enjoy the fly fishing so much, they join the club to continue to grow in the sport.

The financial burden rests on the shoulders of each local retreat, with the approximate cost per participant running around $1,500. The Music City Fly Girls host fundraisers, participate in gift wrapping for donations and accept gifts from sponsors and private individuals on an annual basis. Ask any Music City Fly Girl and she will tell you that, although many hours of hard work and preparation are involved in pulling it all together, the rewards far outweigh the effort and leave us with a tremendous sense of fulfillment.

If you have a chance to join in a retreat as a volunteer or participant, jump at the opportunity. You will find out, firsthand, why I believe that the reward and satisfaction that comes with the warm hug from a thankful participant or a volunteer is far greater than netting that big brown.

CHAPTER 32

European Nymphing

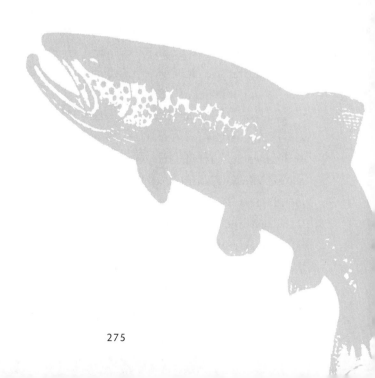

EACH YEAR IN February or early March, the Music City Fly Girls plan an outing to break the cabin fever. We have been cooped up most of the winter, so the group travel is an event to look forward to.

In the past, we have fished the Smoky Mountain streams, but for the past two years, we have planned a trip to fish in Kentucky. The first year was a disappointment because we had to cancel due to extremely high water. The second year, we were getting a repeat of the last. The cabins were booked and the guides secured for float trips on the Cumberland River. However, a call from the guide broke the news I feared would be coming, that the water level was so high it would be treacherous to venture out in the boat. The float trips were obviously canceled.

Instead of disappointing the group for a second year in a row, we decided to take the trip and fish Hatchery Creek instead. One of the main focuses during the group outings is the camaraderie, and with high water or low, we would have a great time.

Hatchery Creek is a man-made stream that flows from Wolf Creek Hatchery to the Cumberland River. It was constructed by the Kentucky Department of Fish & Wildlife Resources in partnership with the U.S. Army Corps of Engineers and U.S. Fish & Wildlife Service. It's a beautiful stretch of water that you would swear had always been there if you didn't know otherwise.

The top section of Hatchery Creek is a catch-and-keep stretch of water. The parklike setting of this area makes it perfect for children or disabled anglers. The remaining stretch of the stream is catch-and-release, allowing artificial tackle only. A man-made stream makes it sound like it would be easy fishing and catching. Well, it's not!

The Music City Fly Girls carpooled to Jamestown, Kentucky, early on a Friday morning to give ample time for fishing once we arrived. We had a larger group than normal on this particular outing, with 25 participating. Our cabins were located at Lake Cumberland State Park— if you haven't been there, you need to make the trip. The cabins are

LEANN WITH A BEAUTIFUL HATCHERY CREEK RAINBOW

economically priced and well kept. The restaurant at Lure Lodge offers a spectacular view of Lake Cumberland, plus delicious food and a friendly waitstaff.

Given the high water on the Cumberland River, Hatchery Creek was also high and stained with the river backing up into the creek, making it almost unrecognizable in some spots. However, we managed to catch our share of fish and didn't regret our decision to make the trip.

Since the club has a number of beginning anglers, we decided to hire a guide to help lead the newcomers along the creek and give some much-needed pointers. Our guide for the day was Troy Humphrey with Cumberland Trout Guide. He did an amazing job working with six of the Fly Girls. The rest of us fished on our own, making our way up and down the creek multiple times throughout the weekend.

This was great exercise, and each evening we looked forward to our group dinners and delicious meals. On our last night together, we all piled into one cabin and hooked the iPad to the television to watch a movie I had downloaded the night before. At the January Music City Fly Girls meeting, Jen Ripple of *Dun Magazine* had given an excellent presentation on the history of women in fly fishing. One name she highlighted, Megan Boyd, left me intrigued; Jen noted a documentary film that had been made about this Scottish woman, a fly tier extraordinaire. I had to have it, so I purchased the film, titled *Kissing the Water,* for the evening's entertainment. I highly recommend this remarkable work of art. We all enjoyed every second of the film.

Our final morning together started out with thunderstorms and heavy rain, so we opted to skip the creek and venture over to the restaurant for breakfast instead. I highly recommend the biscuits and gravy. Another successful Music City Fly Girls outing was in the books.

NECESSARY ACCESSORIES FOR EURO NYMPHING

There are a number of ways to fish Hatchery Creek, but my favorite is using a method called European nymphing. Various techniques were discussed in Chapter 3, including straight-line and indicator nymphing. Euro nymphing, as it's called for short, is simply another

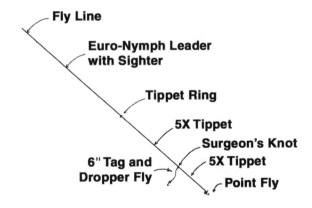

EURO-NYMPHING SETUP

style of nymph fishing. Dry flies and streamers can be used as well, but heavily weighted flies are typically chosen.

The most productive approach to this technique is with a 2- or 3-weight rod that is 10 feet or more in length. Rod companies have started making Euro rods, which are designed with a very sensitive tip. The idea is to keep a tight line through the drift with relatively short casts. In most cases, you don't even cast the fly line. You simply lob the leader and heavily weighted flies upstream with an outstretched arm. Then you allow the flies to travel deep in the water column, keeping the line and leader off the water as you lead the flies downstream with the rod tip.

Specialty Euro fly lines may be purchased; however, since the fly line is rarely used for casting, many fly fishers will use the running line from an old fly line. This is certainly an economical way to get started. The idea when using a thin, level line for the fly line is to keep from allowing your line to sag between the rod guides. If you have any slack in the line, it will be difficult to detect the strike. Attached to the fly line

MOONSHINE EPIPHANY ROD

is a leader, a sighter, a tippet ring, and a straight section of tippet. The sighter is a multicolored tippet material, which serves as the indicator.

My personal setup for this method includes the following:

- Moonshine Epiphany 10-foot, 2-weight rod (moonshinerods.com)

- Airflo Ultralight Euro Nymph fly line (airflousa.com)

- Rio Euro Nymph Leader 2X (the leaders have a white, tapered leader that ends in a two-toned sighter tippet and a tippet ring; rioproducts.com).

After attaching the leader to the fly line, tie a 5X section of tippet to the tippet ring. The length of this section will depend on the depth of the water. Using a surgeon's knot, tie a second piece of 5X tippet, leaving a tag end of about 6 inches. The dropper fly will be attached to the tag end. The point fly is attached to the second section of tippet. There are a number of variations to the setup. I encourage you to explore the options and choose what works for you.

Split shot or twist lead, attached to the leader, typically isn't used in this style of fishing. The weight to get the flies deep into the water column is built into the fly pattern by using tungsten beads and lead wraps. New patterns designed for Euro-style nymphing emerge constantly, once again showing how the learning is endless with fly fishing.

Devin Olsen and Lance Egan, members of Fly Fishing Team USA, have developed two excellent instructional videos, *Modern Nymphing* and *Nymphing Elevated: Beyond the Basics* (tacticalflyfisher.com /books-dvds). The photography is stunning and the guidance is everything you could ask for in getting you started in Euro-style nymphing.

This style of fishing may not be for everyone, but if you like the sensation of being totally connected to your flies and feeling every movement of a fish at the end of the line, then this may be a method you should try. It requires patience and intense focus, but that's exactly what I love about it.

CHAPTER 33

The Missing Chapter: Casting

CASTING ON MY HOME WATERS, THE CANEY FORK RIVER *Photographed by Wade Payne*

WHAT? AN INSTRUCTIONAL fly fishing book and not a single chapter with diagrams and details on how to cast? I know this must be what you are thinking and, yes, it's true. The cast is certainly one of the key components of fly fishing, if not the most important. I contemplated on the best way to approach this topic and have decided on a direction that may surprise you.

There are many books on the market today with excellent write-ups, diagrams, and photographs, each laying out, step by step, how to go about learning the cast. Videos are also available and serve as an excellent supplement to these books. Although these will certainly help, I'm a big believer that there is no substitute for actually doing it. To learn to cast, you need to hold the rod in your hand, feel the weight of the rod as it loads, and experience the sensation of presenting the line with just the right power, speed, and timing. Books and videos will help you refine the cast, but the actual exercise is the real teacher.

With that said, I would like to offer some thoughts on learning to cast based on my years of teaching hundreds of students. These tips, along with hiring a good instructor, some practice, and a good how-to book and video, will get you off to a great start.

Building a Foundation

To start with, don't bite off more than you can chew. The natural tendency is to want to cast the fly line as far as possible and to learn the most advanced casting techniques right away. However, if you can start with the basics and build a solid foundation before jumping too far ahead, then the rest will come naturally.

Roll Cast

The first cast I teach students is the roll cast. It's basically half of the cast, and you will only be casting the line forward. When performed properly, the line, leader, tippet, and fly gracefully roll out on the water. This cast is used for two reasons. First, it helps with casting in tight spots where trees and other obstacles make backcasts difficult or impossible. Second, it helps to set up a cast when the line is puddled in front of you. Before making a basic pickup/backcast, you must have a straight length of line in front of you. Otherwise, the slack will keep the rod from loading properly, leading to a poor casting stroke, wind knots, and other errors. A roll cast will straighten out the line in front of you, giving the best chance possible for making a nice basic cast. I believe the roll cast is one of the most important casts to master.

Basic Cast

Once the roll-cast fundamentals have been established, I will take the student a step further. The basic cast is the classic movement that most people associate with fly fishing. The fly line is peeled from the water and unrolls in a loop behind the caster. Once the line straightens completely, the line is cast forward using the same movement as the roll cast. This is an essential cast needed for fly fishing. All other casts will build upon this cast, so it's critical to work diligently on the technique.

There are key components that make up the cast, and one of the best videos detailing these is by Joan Wulff, titled *Dynamics of Fly Casting*. In the video she unpacks, in great detail, how to properly hold the rod—the proper movement and position of the fingers, wrist, forearm, elbow, and shoulder. It is a great investment, and you should absolutely have this in your fly fishing library. If you have a visual style of learning using diagrams, then the books *Joan Wulff's New Fly-Casting Techniques* and Sheila Hassan's *Fly Casting: A Systematic Approach* are both excellent resources. Whether you are a beginner or advanced fly caster, mastering each of these components will bring your casting to a whole new level.

When I was first learning to cast, I would watch Joan's video religiously, then head out to the field or pond to practice. As nerdy as this sounds, I would set up a video camera on a tripod and record an hour's worth of practice. After the practice, I would bring it home and watch my technique. I would cringe as I could see the rod tip traveling way too far on the backcast, almost touching the ground behind me. As painful as it was to watch, it helped to pick out the various errors that still needed a lot of work.

Common Errors

W<small>E ALL MAKE</small> them. Even some of my students who have fly fished for years have developed bad habits. However, with a few slight adjustments, they improved their casting tremendously. See if any of these common errors might apply to you.

Rod Tip Too High

I <small>OFTEN SEE</small> students starting a cast with the rod tip held parallel to the water surface or even higher. When beginning the basic cast, it's important to keep the rod tip low, almost touching the water. The reason for doing this is to ensure the proper loading of the rod. When the cast begins, the surface tension of the water causes a slight resistance, which in turn bends or loads the fly rod. If the line at the rod tip is off the water, then the load doesn't begin until later in the cast, and the natural tendency is to break the wrist, causing the line to drop to the ground or water behind you.

Too Much Power

It's logical to think that the harder you cast, the farther the line will travel. Nothing could be further from the truth. The secret is to let the rod do all the work. I've seen students put a lot of muscle into their cast, only to see the line kick back at them. To illustrate the softness required, I will stand next to a student and place my hands on theirs and cast with them. I'll ask them not to help with the cast, but simply let their hands ride along as I cast for them to see how gentle the cast should be. They are always amazed that a gentle stroke, with just the right amount of power, will result in the distance they were after.

Incorrect Timing

The time that you pause while the line is unrolling in front of or behind you, during the basic cast, is dependent on the length of line that is outside of the rod tip. If you tend to snap off your flies, or create a popping, whip crack on your forward cast, most likely you are coming forward too quickly and before the line has straightened out behind you. Try turning to the side and watching as your cast unrolls. This will give you an idea of the amount of time needed before starting the forward cast. However, don't get into the habit of always watching your backcast. An occasional glance to see what is behind you when practicing is OK, but it shouldn't be part of your typical casting technique.

Anyone who has taken a class from me knows that I keep a cadence in my head of "one thousand one, one thousand two." Just keep in mind that the cadence will speed up or slow down depending on the amount of line you are casting.

IMPROPER WRIST POSITION

NOTHING WILL DESTROY a cast faster than a sloppy wrist. You have two positions that you should be focused on related to your wrist and how it aligns with the rod butt. At the beginning of the cast, with the rod tip pointed down and close to the water, the wrist will be bent downward, and the rod butt will be parallel or touching the underside of your forearm. It stays in that exact location until you reach the stopping point of your backcast. At that moment, you squeeze the rod to a sudden stop, and the rod will open to a 45-degree angle, and your wrist will be straight, thumb pointed upward. Any farther back will cause the rod tip to drop, and the fly line will follow in a downward trajectory.

On the forward cast, a common error is to let the wrist cock wide open, which tends to resemble more of a throw than a chop. If this sounds familiar to you, the next time you practice, try securing the rod butt under your shirt sleeve. This will help to keep the rod from opening at too wide of an angle. You will feel the pull on your sleeve as you begin to slip back into the bad habit. This is a great practice tool for reminding you about the proper wrist position.

OVERUSING THE FALSE CAST

THE FALSE CAST is the next step in the casting progression after you master the basic cast. This is the aerial, back-and-forth movement of the fly line without stopping. False casting is used for several reasons. It can be used to dry off a fly or strike indicator that has become waterlogged and no longer floats. Casting back and forth will help shake off the water and dry the fly or yarn. This cast can also be used to change the direction or distance of your cast.

False casts should be kept to a minimum—two or three at the most. I've watched new casters false cast over and over before letting the fly finally land on the water. The more time your fly is out of the water, the less time a fish has to eat it.

Ripping Line

I have watched as students begin their backcast by ripping line from the water with all their might in one fell swoop. This makes the line feel like it weighs a ton. Plus, it will scare every fish around and results in a casting disaster. The line should be peeled from the water like a banana. Start out slow and speed up as you go until you reach the line leader connection. Then, with one quick movement, snatch the leader and fly from the water. This approach will be smooth as silk and leave the water completely undisturbed.

Slow Stops

In my opinion, the stop is the most important part of the cast. Once I understood this, my cast improved by leaps and bounds. All too often, I see students start the cast correctly, peeling the line from the water, and then simply slow down to a weak stop. This slow stop will result in a limp line slowly trying to unroll behind you. When I see this, I tell students to "stop like you mean it." The stop should be crisp and abrupt. To help with this, as the student is casting, I will clap my hands together at the time of the stop, signifying how crisp the stop should be. This can be the proverbial light bulb for some students. It definitely was for me. Thanks, Don Jackson, for that lesson many, many years ago!

Practice Makes Perfect

As you practice, here are a few things to keep in mind:

- Practice the roll cast and basic cast with the fly line placed under your index finger. This way you can focus on the various key components without worrying about the line hand.

- Be sure to tie a leader to the end of your fly line when practicing your cast. Casting without a leader could damage your fly line. You may also want to use a small piece of yarn tied to the end of the leader. Using this, along with a target, will help you improve your accuracy.

- Practice in the grass or on the water. Casting on concrete is not recommended because it can damage the fly line.

- Try the video approach I mentioned earlier. You will be amazed at the things you will pick up in your cast. Watch your wrist angle and how your elbow moves. Follow the path of your rod and the stopping point. Is your line unrolling completely? These things will be easy to analyze. I use an app on my smartphone called Coach's Eye. I can zoom in and play it in slow motion.

Beautiful, graceful, artistic. These are all terms that I've heard used to describe fly casting. Beautiful form doesn't just happen overnight. It takes practice to develop the feel and perfect timing that make the cast look effortless and smooth as silk. But it's not just any practice. It needs to be practice using the correct form. If bad form is used and practiced over and over, muscle memory can develop that may be difficult to break. If in doubt, invest in an instructor. Even professional athletes have coaches. Having someone analyze your cast from time to time can help you recognize and correct any bad habits you may be forming. We all need a good tune-up every now and then. Bottom line: Get out there and practice. Don't just read about it or watch videos; practice it for yourself. It's the very best teacher.

CHAPTER 34

Fishing in Canada

THE SUMMER OF 2019 was a first for the Music City Fly Girls in that we had our first ever out-of-the-country trip. When I announced the possibility of the trip at one of our monthly meetings and asked for a show of hands from those who would be interested in going, I was shocked to see so many hands shoot up. In the end, we had 24 excited passengers headed to Calgary, Alberta, for an exciting adventure.

I started planning the trip in early January to be sure we could lock in our hotel reservations, grab some reasonably priced airfares, and pick up 12 fly fishing guides.

After a little research, I selected Doug Massig of Bow River Fly Fishing to work with us in scheduling our wade and float trips. He did an excellent job answering all of my questions, patiently making adjustments to our plans, and arranging all the guides to lead this large group of anglers. Given the group size, he pulled a number of guides from other shops, and it was just what we needed.

We decided to stay at the Delta Hotels Calgary South, a Marriott property, and it was one of the best decisions of the trip-planning process. The hotel was perfect for our group. They had a beautiful lobby with plenty of room to sit and visit, delicious and well-priced meals, and some of the best customer service any of us have ever experienced.

OUR LEAD GUIDE, DOUG MASSIG, WITH ROLINDA BEFORE HEADING TO FLOAT THE BOW RIVER

The rooms were nicely furnished and large enough for our typical "four to a room" travel protocol.

That evening, we drove into downtown Calgary for a group dinner at the Palomino Smokehouse, a restaurant known for its smoked meats. We walked into the rustic little joint and felt right at home when we spotted the enormous mural of Johnny Cash hanging on the wall. We enjoyed the atmosphere, friendly servers, and every single bite of the four "Fat A— Platters," a restaurant specialty we ordered to share.

Our guides arrived to pick us up early the next morning for our first full day of Canadian fishing. We split up, four to a guide, and went our separate ways, promising to return for dinner and some fish stories. It was a 2-hour trek into the mountains to reach two of Alberta's top cutthroat streams, the Oldman and the Livingstone. Both are catch-and-release rivers with average trout ranging in length from 13 to 16 inches. The rivers are open from June through October, so arriving in August was perfect. I've heard many times that the journey is as good as the destination, and this was certainly the case for us. The scenery along the way was spectacular, and our guides were very gracious in letting us stop along the way for some quick photos.

SUSAN, ANGIE, AND CHARLEY STOPPING ALONG THE WAY TO POSE WITH THE BEAUTIFUL SCENERY IN THE BACKGROUND

IT WAS EASY WADING IN THE LIVINGSTONE.

Once we arrived, however, we got down to business and spent the day walking up and down the rivers. We were pleasantly surprised to see that we had the water all to ourselves. These rivers don't seem to get much fishing pressure, especially in the middle of the week. We found the river to be very safe and easy to wade. I caught myself stopping numerous times to look around and take in the sights. The water was clear, and the color was almost tropical.

I was in the group guided by Paul Laframboise, an excellent guide who spends many days each year on the Canadian waters. He is in high demand, so we felt fortunate to have him show us the ropes on the Livingstone.

The technique used for the majority of the day was nymph fishing under an indicator and Euro nymphing. We landed a number of beautiful cutthroat trout and left the river feeling very satisfied. The groups fished various sections of the Livingstone and the Oldman, and all had wonderful experiences.

We had a long drive back to the hotel, which gave us plenty of time to pepper the guides with questions about the Bow River, where we would be floating the next two days. We learned that the Bow River has a 50-mile stretch of blue-ribbon water with 3,000 fish per mile. It's full of rainbow and brown trout, which, although not indigenous, are self-sustaining. The best times to fish are May, July, August, September and October, with June being the month for snowmelt and runoff. Again, we found August to be the perfect time for us.

The weather wasn't as kind to us the next day as we ventured out for our first float on the Bow River. As the guides pulled up to the hotel with drift boats in tow, the cloud cover was building, and we fished in a downpour the majority of the morning. However, the fish were still eating, so we picked up a few. It was a long, wet day, but no one complained.

The second day's weather was much better, and we had a large dose of sunshine. There was significant rainfall the day before, so the high water made the fish a little tight-lipped, but we enjoyed every minute. My guide for the second day was also named Paul, Paul Grindlay. He turned out to be not only an excellent guide, but an opera singer and a poet as well (he wrote the poem on page iv). He served a delicious lunch, recited an original poem, and treated us to some excellent conversation and facts about the river. It was one of the best days on the water that I can remember.

CHARLEY WITH HER FIRST CUTTHROAT

ANGIE (PICTURED WITH OUR OPERA-SINGING GUIDE, PAUL) LANDED A BEAUTIFUL RAINBOW ON A DRY FLY CAST PERFECTLY AGAINST THE BANK.

Our final day in Canada was spent doing a little sightseeing around the Canadian Rockies. We enjoyed high tea at the Fairmont Chateau Lake Louise, a walk around the lake, and a little shopping as we toured downtown Banff. This was, indeed, one of the best trips the Music City Fly Girls have taken in our 12 years of traveling.

If you decide to venture out on a similar trip, here are a few things to keep in mind:

- You will need a passport. It used to be a birth certificate would work, but this isn't the case anymore.

- Order your Canadian currency two weeks before departure. The bank doesn't keep a supply on hand.

- Check the exchange rate. During our trip, the exchange was in our favor, and it was like getting the trip 40% off!

- You can expect to pay 5% GST (Goods and Services Tax).

- Calgary is on Mountain Time, so the jet lag is minimal.

- Check with your insurance company about renting a car in Canada. Mine sent me a special card to keep with the car.

- Travel insurance is inexpensive and is always a good idea.

- Fishing licenses are available online with one-day and seven-day options available.

- Be sure to talk with your bank and cell phone provider about a travel card and data coverage to avoid international fees.

- You can plan on Uber and Lyft being available to get around downtown Calgary.

- Fly rods in the 5- or 6-weight range work perfectly.

If you haven't been out of the country, Canada is a great way to start. The people are very friendly, it's easy to get around, the exchange rate works in our (US) favor, and the scenery is amazing.

THE GROUP BY LAKE LOUISE AFTER HIGH TEA

Winding It Up

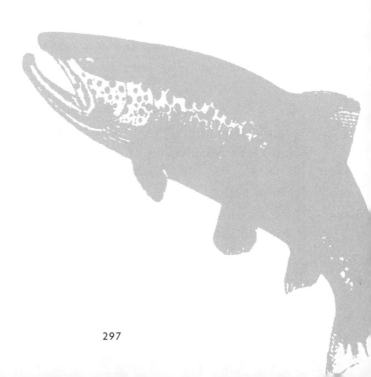

As I write the following conclusion to this book, I'm filled with a sense of satisfaction on many levels. Of course, the one that is obvious is to have completed each of the chapters contained in my original outline as scheduled. However, the greater satisfaction goes far beyond meeting a deadline.

When I was first contemplating the writing of this book, I called Joan to talk with her about it and to get her thoughts. One of the things she told me would happen was something she had experienced with her first book. She predicted that before writing on a topic, I would study it thoroughly and in the process, I would increase my own knowledge significantly. She was exactly right. This has happened without a doubt. Things that I thought I understood, or topics on which I had only limited knowledge, I've come to learn in much greater detail. Once again, I've been reminded that fly fishing is a life-long learning experience. I will never know it all!

Over the many months it's taken to flesh out the outline I initially created, I have relived some humbling moments I experienced along my fly fishing journey. The day on the South Holston River with my dad and Robert, when I was casting so awkwardly but still managed to land that life-changing trout, seems like yesterday. It's also brought me to the realization that I've come a long way since then. I've experienced different rivers, different fishing conditions and techniques, made countless friends, and met some of the legends of the fly fishing world. The blessings continue to flow my way, and I am so thankful.

At this moment, while finishing this book, The Music City Fly Girls are finalizing plans for a weeklong trip to Wyoming. We have a full house with 39 members already securing their deposits. We will be staying on the Shoshone River and plan to visit Yellowstone Park and the Grand Tetons. You can be sure our eyes will be watching for the white feathers that are certain to line our path.

I was taken by surprise at the clarity of the memories I have of all the wonderful travel adventures with the Music City Fly Girls. With the club in its 12th year, you would think that some of the details would have faded, but that wasn't the case. I'm so grateful the members continue to trust me to lead them each year to new and exciting places to fish.

WE WILL ALWAYS BE WATCHING FOR WHITE FEATHERS. THANK YOU, NIKKI!

Glossary

- **ARBOR** The center of the reel spool, around which the backing and the fly line are wound. Reels come in three arbor sizes: standard, medium, and large. The larger the arbor, the faster you can retrieve the fly line.

- **ATTRACTOR** A fly that doesn't imitate anything in nature and is typically tied with flash and bright colors such as purple or pink. It is widely believed the fish will take the fly out of curiosity.

- **BACKCAST** The backcast happens during the cast when the rod stops slightly off vertical, and the line is propelled behind the caster.

- **BACKING** Made of Dacron or polyester, the backing is the slender line tied directly to the arbor of the reel and then attached to the fly line. It serves two purposes: It bulks up the spool diameter so the line isn't wound too tightly around the spool reel itself, resulting in tight coils. It also serves as insurance. A typical fly line is 90 feet long. If you hook into a large fish that takes off running on you and takes out all 90 feet of line, then you may be out of luck without the extra length of attached backing to continue fighting the fish.

- **BARB** A sharp section of the hook projecting at an upward angle from the hook point. It is used to help hold the fish to the hook, making extraction more difficult.

- **BARBLESS** A hook with the barb mashed down or one that has been manufactured without a barb.

- **BEAD HEAD** A bead tied to the hook when creating a fly pattern to increase weight or to add flash to the fly.

- **BLOOD KNOT** A slim-profile knot used to tie two pieces of line together, such as leader to tippet. The two lines should be of similar size or no greater than .002 inch in diameter. It is also known as a barrel knot.

- **BOBBIN** A tool that holds fly-tying thread.

- **BUMP** The feel of a fish moving against your fly but not actually committing to eating the fly.

- **BUTT SECTION** A butt section has bulb-shaped corks located at the bottom of the rod, which help to secure the rod against your waist while fighting the fish.

- **CATCH AND RELEASE** Gently releasing a fish after it is caught. This is a practice used by a large majority of fly fishers.

- **COMPLETE METAMORPHOSIS** Complete metamorphosis is when an insect goes through the four distinct stages of its life cycle: the egg, larva, pupa, and adult. The adult takes on a completely different form than the immature insect, as in the transformation of a caterpillar into a butterfly.

- **DEAD DRIFT** Allowing the current to move the fly with no motion imparted by the angler.

- **DENIER** A standard of measurement relating to the mass in grams of 9,000 meters of thread. The most common sizes for fly-tying thread are 70, 140, and 210 denier.

- **DOUBLE HAUL** An advanced casting technique where the line hand pulls on the line at the stop, increasing the line speed.

- **DOUBLE TAPER** A fly line with a front taper, belly, and rear taper, with no running line.

- **DRAG** The unnatural motion imparted to the fly as the current catches and pulls the fly line, leader, or strike indicator downstream ahead of the fly.

- **DRIFT** The follow-through after the stop on the backcast. Drift is used to increase the stroke length, allowing for a deeper loading of the rod. It can also be used to describe the natural movement of the fly or strike indicator in the water.

● **DRIFT BOAT** A dory-type vessel used to float rivers. The typical setup is a casting brace for anglers in the front and back of the boat to help them stay balanced when standing. There is also a spot in the center of the boat for the person rowing. Oars are mounted in oar locks on each side of the boat. Drift boats are designed to float in very shallow water with their wide, flat bottoms and flared sides.

● **DROPPER** A trailing fly tied after or below the point fly.

● **DRY FLY** A fly pattern created with buoyant material, allowing it to float on the water's surface.

● **DUBBING** Fly-tying material that is spun onto thread and wrapped around a hook to imitate a fly or other insect. It can be made of natural fur and hair or synthetic materials, which come in a variety of textures and colors.

● **DUN** The immature stage of a mayfly between the nymph and adult; also known as subimago. During this stage, the wings are dull or opaque. Also the name of a great fly fishing magazine, helmed by Editor-in-Chief Jen Ripple.

● **EDDY** The circular movement of water in the opposite direction of the main current, typically created behind a rock or other obstruction.

● **EMERGER** The stage in an insect's life cycle when it hatches or begins to shed its outer skeleton, and the winged adult begins to emerge.

● **EUROPEAN NYMPHING** A tight-line method of fly fishing in which a long rod is used to extend the reach and a multicolored section of monofilament within the leader is used to detect strikes and determine water depth. This section is known as a sighter and replaces the traditional strike indicator. Heavily weighted flies are used instead of lead or split shot to ensure flies are fished deep in the water column.

• **FALSE CAST** Casting back and forth in the air to dry off a fly, lengthen the amount of line outside the rod tip, or change the direction of the cast.

• **FLOATANT** A clear, gel-like substance applied to a dry fly that works to keep the fly from absorbing water, which in turn helps with floating the fly.

• **FLUOROCARBON** A plastic used for leaders and tippets that has properties that make it invisible to the fish. It has a higher density and is more abrasion resistant than nylon-based monofilament. It is also significantly more expensive.

• **FOAM LINE** Small bubbles of air collecting on the surface of the water that can trap emerging or drowned insects. The foam serves as cover or camouflage for fish, and this, along with the trapped insects, forms attractive areas where fish will congregate. This is why the phrase "foam is home" is often used.

• **FOUL HOOK** Hooking the fish in a part of the body other than the lip or mouth.

• **FREESTONE** A stream formed by snowmelt or rainfall, with water levels fluctuating with the seasons.

• **GRAVEL GUARDS** Cuffs worn around the tops of boots to keep small stones and pebbles from getting inside.

• **HACKLE** Feather from the neck or back of a chicken raised specifically for its fly-tying feathers.

• **HACKLE PLIERS** A tool used in fly tying to hold feathers as they are being wound around the hook.

- **HEMOSTATS** A tool similar to snub-nosed scissors that is used to remove a hook from a fish or mash the barbs on a hook. They are also called forceps.

- **HOOK SET** The motion of the rod or line used to move the hook into place and penetrate the mouth of the fish.

- **HOPPER DROPPER** A tandem rig where the point fly is a grasshopper imitation followed by a trailing nymph such as a bead-head pheasant tail.

- **IMPROVED CLINCH KNOT** A common knot used to attach the fly to the end of the tippet.

- **INCOMPLETE METAMORPHOSIS** The development of an insect going through three distinct stages: egg, nymph, and adult. The insect looks the same in its immature form as it does in the adult form, with one exception: the adult has wings.

- **INDICATOR** A floating piece of line, yarn, or other device attached to the leader that allows the angler to detect a strike.

- **LARVA** An early stage of insect development preceding complete metamorphosis to winged adult.

- **LDR (LONG DISTANCE RELEASE)** A term used when the fish gets off before you have a chance to bring it to the net.

- **LEADER** A length of nylon or fluorocarbon line attached to the end of the fly line. It is tapered and sized to match the fly being used. Leaders can either be knotless or manually knotted. Knotless leaders are manufactured to taper down smoothly, whereas knotted leaders are tapered by manually, adding various diameters of tippet material down to the desired size.

- **LEVEL LINE** A fly line with a constant diameter.

- **LILLIAN** A short piece of line built into the end of a tenkara rod where the line or leader is attached.

- **LOAD** The bending of the fly rod.

- **LOOP-TO-LOOP CONNECTION** The joining of two lines with loops in each end, forming an interlocking connection.

- **MENDING** Adjusting the fly line on the water to ensure the fly floats, drifts, or swims naturally in the water.

- **MIDGE** A two-winged insect resembling a mosquito that goes through a complete metamorphosis. They are relatively small flies, which leads anglers to use this term when referring to tiny insects or fly imitations.

- **MONOFILAMENT** A nylon-based line used for leaders and tippets. It has a lower density than fluorocarbon, making it ideal for top-water applications. It is also more visible and relatively cheap.

- **NAIL KNOT** Typically used to attach the backing (and the leader) to the fly line. A nail knot tool or other device is used as a guide to assist in threading the line during the tying process.

- **NIPPERS** Small tools used to snip pieces of tippet.

- **NYMPH** A stage in insect development as it gradually changes to an adult through incomplete metamorphosis. The nymph resembles the adult, without the wings.

- **OVER-LINING** Using a line weight that is heavier than what the rod is designed to carry.

- **PERFECTION LOOP** A nonslip knot that is typically tied at the end of the leader and then used to attach the fly line with a loop-to-loop connection.

- **POINT FLY** The first fly that is tied to the end of the tippet.

- **POOL** A relatively deep section of a body of water where the current is slow-moving.

- **PUPAE** A stage of complete metamorphosis when the insect is transforming into an adult.

- **REACH CAST** A casting technique used to make an aerial mend so the line lands upstream of the fly.

- **REDD** A scooped-out area in the rocks where a fish deposits eggs.

- **RIFFLE** A fast-moving, shallow stretch of water flowing over rocks, causing rough or nervous water.

- **ROLL CAST** A casting technique used when obstructions or slack line prevents a backcast. The line is cast forward in a loop and rolls out on the water to present the fly.

- **SEAM** A place in a river or stream where slow and fast currents come together, forming a visible joining line.

- **SHANK** The straight section of the hook immediately behind the hook eye.

- **SHORT STRIKE** When a fish takes the material of the fly, such as the tail, but misses the hook.

- **SINK TIP** A fly line with a floating section over the majority of the line and a sinking section at the tip, typically 10–20 feet. The sinking section may be integrated into the fly line or attached with a loop-to-loop connection.

- **SPLIT SHOT** A round piece of lead with a slit through the center. The tippet is placed in the slit a few inches above the fly, and the lead is pinched closed around the tippet with hemostats. The added weight allows the fly to drop to the desired depth. Split shot is offered in various sizes depending on the speed of the current and how quickly you need to reach depth.

- **SPRING CREEK** A creek where the water source is an underground aquifer.

- **STREAMER** A fly tied to represent a baitfish, crayfish, or leech.

- **STRIKE INDICATOR** A strike indicator is an item or color used on the leader to detect when a fish takes the fly. Strike indicators can be made out of yarn, adhesive foam, plastic, or simply a change of color on the leader.

- **STRIPPING** A motion imparted to the fly by pulling in the fly line with the line hand.

- **STROKE LENGTH** The distance your casting hand moves during the casting stroke.

- **SURGEON'S KNOT** Used to tie lines of equal or unequal sizes together, typically when tying leader to tippet.

- **TAILING LOOP** A common casting error where the leader and fly drop below the bottom leg of the casting loop. Often this results in a knot or tangle.

- **TAIL OUT** The downstream end of a pool as it flows out to a shallower section of the river or stream.

- **TAILWATER** A body of water located downstream of a dam.

- **TENKARA** A Japanese method of fly fishing where only a rod, line, and fly are used. There is no reel attached to the rod. The line or leader is attached to a lillian, or a short piece of line built into the rod.

- **"TIGHT LINES"** A greeting between fly fishers, meaning good luck. When you hook a fish, your line goes tight.

- **TIPPET** The end of the leader that attaches to the fly. On a manufactured tapered leader, it's the thinnest section at the tip end. Tippet material can be purchased in spools to build or repair leaders.

- **TIPPET GAUGE** A small tool with notches that is used to measure tippet size.

- **TIPPET RING** A tiny metal ring that serves as a connection point between the leader and tippet material. This is an optional method used instead of tying leader and tippet together using a surgeon's or blood knot.

- **TWIST LEAD** A supple, flat lead that is twisted around the leader or tippet to assist in getting the fly deeper in the water. This is an alternative to split shot.

- **UNDER-LINING** Using a line weight that is lighter than what the rod is designed to carry.

- **WEIGHT FORWARD** A fly-line design with most of the weight in the forward section, or first 30–40 feet of the overall fly line.

- **WET FLY** A fly, typically fished in the surface film, that represents an emerging insect and is typically tied with soft hackles.

- **WHIP-FINISH TOOL** A tool used to help tie off the thread when making flies.

- **X DIAMETER** A system of measurement used to identify the diameter of tippet, with 0X (.011 inch) being the largest and 8X (.003 inch) being the smallest.

Resources and
Contact Information

Below you will find contact information for all the resources mentioned in this guide.

Clubs and Charities

Casting for Recovery
castingforrecovery.org

Music City Fly Girls
Nashville, TN
musiccityflygirls.com

Tennessee's Wild Side **Middle Tennessee Casting for Recovery Retreat**
youtu.be/6ICQ4SFfo6Q

Fishing Spots and Schedules

Caney Fork River
Center Hill Dam Tailwater Release Schedule
tva.gov/Environment/Lake-Levels/Center-Hill

Dry Run Creek
arkansas.com/fishing-spot/dry-run-creek

Elk River Generation Schedule
tva.gov/Environment/Lake-Levels/Tims-Ford

Hatchery Creek
fw.ky.gov/Fish/Pages/Hatchery-Creek-Stream.aspx

Lake Cumberland State Park
parks.ky.gov/parks/resortparks/lake-cumberland

Rock Creek
monocounty.org/places-to-go/lakes-rivers-creeks/rock-creek

Guided Trips

Cumberland Trout Guide
Jamestown, KY
859-494-4489; cumberlandtroutguide.com

David Perry, Southeastern Fly
Middle Tennessee
615-796-5143; southeasternfly.com

Doug Massig, Bow River Fly Fishing
Calgary and Banff, AB
403-470-3474; bowriverflyfishing.com

Matt Millner, Rising River Guides
White River, AR
501-691-9285; matt@risingriverguides.com

Paul Grindlay
Alberta, CA
403-990-6094

Paul Laframboise, Iron Bow Fly Shop & Outfitters
Calgary, AB
403-478-8313; trouthunterpaul@gmail.com
ironbowflyshop.com

Reel Women
Victor, ID
reelwomenflyfishing.com

Tight Line Adventures
Dillon, MT
406-925-1684; tightlinemontana.com/guided-fishing

Lessons
Fly Fishers International (FFI)
406-222-9369; flyfishersinternational.org

Orvis
orvis.com/ff101

Southern Brookies
Lancaster, TN
615-627-7850; southernbrookies.com

Wulff School of Fly Fishing
Lew Beach, NY
845-439-5020; wulffschool.com

Lodging and Restaurants
The Arctic Club Seattle, a DoubleTree by Hilton Hotel
700 Third Ave., Seattle, WA
206-340-0340; tinyurl.com/thearcticclubseattle

Beaverkill Valley Inn
7 Barnhart Road, Lew Beach, NY
845-439-4844; beaverkillvalleyinn.com

Best Western Rocky Mountain Lodge
6510 US 93 S, Whitefish, MT
800-780-7234; tinyurl.com/bestwesternrml

Campfire Lodge
155 Campfire Lane, West Yellowstone, MT
406-646-7258; campfirelodgewestyellowstone.com

Casa Brava
701 W. Kingshighway, Paragould, AR
870-240-8363

Chick's Café
154 S. Main St., Heber City, UT
435-654-1771

Crowley Lake Fish Camp
1149 S. Landing Road; Mammoth Lakes, CA
Front Gate: 760-935-4043
Tackle Shop: 760-935-4301
crowleylakefishcamp.com

Delta Hotels Calgary South
135 Southland Drive SE, Calgary, AB
403-278-5050
marriott.com/hotels/travel/yycdc-delta-hotels-calgary-south

Fairmont Chateau Lake Louise (high tea)
111 Lake Louise Drive, Lake Louise, AB
855-479-0732; fairmont.com/lake-louise

Fisheads San Juan River Lodge
1796 NM 173, Navajo Dam, NM
505-634-0463; fisheadsofthesanjuan.com

Hinkle Hill Inn
Bell Buckle, TN
615-429-8629; hinklehillinn.com

Hotel Glenwood Springs
52000 Two Rivers Plaza Road, Glenwood Springs, CO
888-411-8188; thehotelglenwoodsprings.com

Kimpton Hotel Monaco
506 SW Washington St., Portland, OR
503-222-0001; monaco-portland.com

Long Branch Campground
478 Lancaster Road, Lancaster, TN
615-548-8002; recreation.gov/camping/campgrounds/232630

Palomino Smokehouse
109 Seventh Ave. SW, Calgary, AB
403-532-1911; thepalomino.ca

PJ's Lodge & River Run Restaurant
384 Lodge Lane, Norfork, AR
877-761-7575; pjslodge.com

Riverside Motel
346 Main St., Ennis, MT
406-682-4240; riversidemotel-outfitters.com

Riverside Retreat
205 River Valley Trail, Norfork, AR
870-499-0694; whiteriverresort.com

Stumptown Coffee Roasters
stumptowncoffee.com

Swiss Alps Inn
167 S. Main St., Heber City, UT
435-654-0722; swissalpsinn.com

Tom's Place
8180 Crowley Lake Drive, Crowley Lake, CA
760-935-4239; tomsplaceresort.com

Voodoo Doughnut
voodoodoughnut.com

Other Resources

Animated Knots
animatedknots.com

Coach's Eye app
coachseye.com

Dun Magazine
dunmagazine.com

Fishing Licenses, Alberta
albertarelm.com

Gratuity Guidelines for Guided Trips
orvis.com/s/gratuity-guidelines-for-fishing-guides-and-staff/14926

Tim Flagler, Tightline Productions, LLC (fly-tying videos)
tightlinevideo.com; practicalpatterns.com (YouTube channel)

Team App
teamapp.com

Website Creation
register.com

Outfitters

Airflo Fly Line
airflousa.com for retailers

Cumberland Transit
2807 West End Ave., Nashville, TN
615-321-4069; cumberlandtransit.com

Dally's Ozark Fly Fisher
1200 W. Main, #7, Cotter, AR
870-435-6166; theozarkflyfisher.com

Jackson Adventures
931-738-4800; jacksonkayak.com

Lakestream Fly Shop
669 Spokane Ave., Whitefish, MT
406-862-1298; lakestream.com

Moonshine Fly Rods
moonshinerods.com

Northwest Flies
2203 SE 184th Ave., Portland, OR; greatflies.com

Rio Products
206-780-8789; rioproducts.com/freshwater/leader

Scotty Equipment
800-214-0141; scotty.com

Temple Fork Outfitters
tforods.com

Tenkara USA
888-1-TENKARA (483-6527); tenkarausa.com

Tenkara Bum
tenkarabum.com

Tim's Flies and Lies Outfitters
(call for appointment and shuttle service)
384 Flowertown Road, Normandy, TN
931-759-5058; Rhonda Page: 931-607-3645; timsfliesandlies.com

Trout Bum 2
4343 N. UT 224, Ste. 101, Park City, UT
435-658-1166; troutbum2.com

Transportation

Amtrak *California Zephyr*
amtrak.com/california-zephyr-train

Amtrak *Empire Builder*
amtrak.com/empire-builder-train

Roaring Fork Transportation Authority
Transportation to Aspen from Glenwood Springs, CO
rfta.com/routes/system-map

Index

DEAR CUSTOMERS AND FRIENDS,

SUPPORTING YOUR INTEREST IN OUTDOOR ADVENTURE, travel, and an active lifestyle is central to our operations, from the authors we choose to the locations we detail to the way we design our books. Menasha Ridge Press was incorporated in 1982 by a group of veteran outdoorsmen and professional outfitters. For many years now, we've specialized in creating books that benefit the outdoors enthusiast.

Almost immediately, Menasha Ridge Press earned a reputation for revolutionizing outdoors- and travel-guidebook publishing. For such activities as canoeing, kayaking, hiking, backpacking, and mountain biking, we established new standards of quality that transformed the whole genre, resulting in outdoor-recreation guides of great sophistication and solid content. Menasha Ridge Press continues to be outdoor publishing's greatest innovator.

The folks at Menasha Ridge Press are as at home on a whitewater river or mountain trail as they are editing a manuscript. The books we build for you are the best they can be, because we're responding to your needs. Plus, we use and depend on them ourselves.

We look forward to seeing you on the river or the trail. If you'd like to contact us directly, visit us at menasharidge.com. We thank you for your interest in our books and the natural world around us all.

SAFE TRAVELS,

Bob Sehlinger

BOB SEHLINGER
PUBLISHER

About the Author

S USAN THRASHER STARTED fishing at a young age with her dad in East Tennessee and has been passionate about the outdoors all her life. In 2004, she started Southern Brookies Fly Fishing, a guide

THE JACKSON SUPERFISHAL SETUP
Photographed by Nonie Sanders

service and instructional school based in Nashville, Tennessee. She left a successful engineering career in 2015 to venture into the business full time. Her passion for fly fishing led her to serve as the cofounder of the Music City Fly Girls, a women's fly fishing club, and to serve as the Middle Tennessee retreat leader for Casting for Recovery, a nonprofit organization focused on breast cancer survivors and the healing nature of fly fishing. Susan credits most of her teaching success with experience gained as an instructor at the Joan Wulff School of Fly Fishing, where she has been on staff for the past 15 years. She currently lives in East Nashville, Tennessee, just a short drive from her beloved Caney Fork River.